MO
HEADE

# Nothing Shall Separate Me

## From Despair to Deliverance

Studio Griffin
A Publishing Company
www.studiogriffin.net

For information, contact:
Studio Griffin
A Publishing Company
Garner, North Carolina
studiogriffin@outlook.com
www.studiogriffin.net

Cover Design by Ruth E. Griffin
Image by © Monique Headecker-Green

First Edition

ISBN-13: 978-1-954818-20-0

Library of Congress Control Number: 2021906315

Printed in the U.S.A.

1 2 3 4 5 6 7 8 9 10

To my children, Tyrell and Damien, for giving me a reason to fight the many obstacles I faced. For being there for me and always feeding me positive words when I was fighting for my life, and for not letting me give up. No matter what I went through, looking into the faces of my children and into their beautiful eyes, gave me the will to live and to learn what my purpose was.

To my beautiful mother, Janet, who has gone on to be with the Lord. Thank you for living every day with a purpose. Thank you for teaching your daughters how to be ladies. You instilled in me morals, integrity, love and doing things with a spirit of excellence. You were an example of what it takes to make it as a single mother raising three children on your own. I pray that I make you proud.

To my sister, Lisa, who is the epitome of what a hard worker is. You were definitely my role model. You may have never known that because I never told you. Today I tell you, you set a great example as an older sister. Thank you also to your better half, your husband, my brother-in-love, John, for loving my sister, and loving her sister and children like your own.

To my brother, Howard. Thank you for loving your big sis even though I stayed on you like a mother. You are a great man. I love you.

Last but not least, to my husband, Emmanuel. What can I say? Much, but I will just say this: Thank you for hanging in there and sticking and staying through the good and the bad. Thank you for honoring your vows and being faithful to not me, but God. Thank you for showing me what real love is from a man. I love you with everything that is in me.

# Table of Contents

# Nothing Shall Separate Me

## From Despair to Deliverance

# Introduction

I wrote this book for every woman and man who has found themselves in a place of brokenness, confusion, and instability. This book was written so that women and men would choose to live in a place of authenticity and get their lives back by living in truth and not being ashamed of what they have been through.

We all go through things in life that we are not proud of or are ashamed to talk about. Some things are little, while others are big; some things are sad, happy, tragic, or joyous. I want my readers to know that no matter what we have been through, God is ever-present, speaking, leading, guiding, and still delivering us out of chaos into Kairos.

My prayer is that you are encouraged and inspired to change your mindset, start speaking things into existence, changing your thoughts from negative to positive, to be motivated and live in the moment, and not let your circumstances dictate how you live your life. I want everyone to live their best life, to live a limitless life so that they can be free and soar to the places that God has already planned for them!

Part 1

# Experiencing
# and Experimenting

Monique Headecker-Green

# Chapter 1

I started my journey into young adulthood, at the age of fourteen, hanging out with a couple of friends and trying new things. The first thing I experimented with was cigarettes. I don't exactly remember how or where I got my first cigarette, but I think it was from my girlfriend who lived downstairs in our apartment building. We would go into the staircase of our building, all the way up to the last floor near the rooftop, and we would have fun puffing. That was the start of a habit that I wish that I never indulged in. I believe that after the second week of sneaking wherever we could to go and smoke cigarettes, I was already hooked.

I found myself sneaking cigarettes from family members who smoked when they left the room. I even remember asking a family friend when she came over to my house one day, if I could have a puff when she lit one up.

"What are you talking about, 'Can I have a puff?'" she asked.

I told her, "I smoke!"

But she said, "No, you are not going to get me in trouble!"

"My mother knows that I smoke," I insisted. Mind you, my mom was in the other room, and she did not know at the time that I was dipping and dabbing in cigarettes. Nevertheless, I persisted, and when that didn't work, I went back to sneaking them.

I found myself liking boys at that time as well. I was now fifteen years old, and I had eyes only for one guy specifically—Antwon. I could not get him off my mind. We started seeing one another. He was one of those pretty boys that all the girls wanted. He was a player with good hair and light skin. He may have been mixed with Asian because he had narrow eyes. He was actually prettier than me! Antwon was also into girls and sexually active at the time. I wasn't though, I was still a virgin. Although I was in love with him and I wanted him to be my first, I felt like I couldn't do it. I was too scared. I can't remember my mother ever sitting me down discussing sex with me; I thought it was a painful thing and I sure didn't want to become a young mother. Being with a young, sexually active male was not easy for a virgin, young lady, and it was hard for a young man who had already sowed his oats. It was a hard relationship to maintain. This caused cheating and unfaithfulness on his part. I guess I could not blame him, because like he said, he was a male and he had his needs. Although I sure wanted my first experience to be with him, I wasn't willing to meet those needs. So, we had to part ways.

The break-up was very painful for me. It was my first encounter with depression. I don't believe my family was aware of it though, as I covered it up very well. The only person I shared what I was going through with this guy was my aunt. Sometimes it's not good to tell your family or friends about a boyfriend or what you are going through. When you're hurt, you do nothing but discuss all the negative things about the person and they end up not liking that person. That was my first taste of 'keep your relationship problems to yourself.'

I tried my best to keep my mind off what I was going through, so I would hang out with my friends in the back of their building, and we would play cards all night. We would chip in and buy Heineken beer. I was not a drinker and didn't indulge in it much, it always tasted nasty to me. But I did not want to be the weak link in the bunch either. I don't think they would have cared one way or another whether I had a beer or not, it was more for them, but this was probably more me not wanting them to think I was boring.

Despite that, when I smoked a cigarette, I didn't mind having a beer. After a few sips, I was what you called tipsy. I called it drunk. I remember drinking a whole can of Budweiser one time and being gone. My friends asked me, "How can you get drunk off one beer, and the wateriest beer at that?"

I guess if you're not a drinker that's what happens. It doesn't take much.

One of my girlfriends was named Zelma. I grew up with her in the projects and she hung out in the back of our apartment building with me. Zelma's mom, Mama Butler, was into church. I would always hang out at their house, and one day her mom invited me to go to church with them. I said, "Sure."

I didn't grow up in church. I can't recall my mom going when we were growing up, but I do remember always wanting to make it to church on Palm Sunday to get my palms. I remember going to Blessed Sacrament Church sometimes. It was a Catholic Church not too far from where we lived. My sister and I would go and get our palms.

I think ultimately, though, deep down inside I always wanted to give church a try. I have always felt like I wanted to know who this God was that my girlfriend's mother spoke so highly of. I remember when I went with them for the first time, I found myself loving the experience. I loved the singing and even the preaching. I recall seeing a lady jump out of her chair and start jumping around and screaming and saying, "Hallelujah." I didn't know what that was, and I think I was as scared as I was fascinated.

I asked Mama Butler after church what was wrong with that lady who jumped out of the chair and started screaming. She told me that she was filled with the Holy Ghost and the word witnessed to her spirit. She told me that when you give your life to Christ, start reading His word and building a relationship with Him, He will fill you with His Holy Spirit. Sometimes, when that word is in you and it agrees with what is being preached, that will happen to you. I wanted to go to church more just to hear the singing, preaching and what they called shouting, because deep down inside I wanted to experience that myself. I didn't go every Sunday with them, but I went here and there.

# Chapter 2

One day, my best friend, Lia, and I decided we would hang out together since her family was out of town. When the evening came, we agreed that we would get a bag of weed and go to the house, smoke, listen to some music and have a good ole time. We proceeded to go to a lady's house named Grandma to purchase the marijuana. Personally, I couldn't believe that there was a lady that was up there in age (probably around sixty-something) selling weed out of her house, but I was only sixteen at the time. I was still young and naive. We were nervous to go in, so we sent a guy I knew to get it for us. He was going in anyway, so he didn't mind doing that.

When he came out, we went back to Lia's house, turned on some music and rolled our joint as best we could. We weren't everyday smokers—I could count on both hands how many times I indulged in smoking weed. But I liked how mellow weed made me feel afterward, so when I got the chance to smoke it, I did. What I did not like was that it gave you the munchies and made your eyes red and half closed, which was a dead giveaway that you were smoking if you were trying to hide that fact from anyone.

After we finished smoking, I lit up a cigarette. We turned the music up and were dancing and enjoying ourselves.

Not too long after that, I started feeling bad. My heart began racing, and it felt like a jack hammer was pounding in my chest. I grabbed onto my friend and told her what I was feeling. I thought if I sat down on the bed and calmed down, things would go back to normal. But then I started breathing fast and panicking. My heart proceeded to pound out of my chest. We were both nervous and didn't know what was going on or what to do. I didn't want to go home and have my mother find out what I was doing. I told Lia that we needed to sneak in my house, get my sister and tell her.

We arrived at my home and woke up my sister. She put on her clothes and together we decided we would walk around outside and get some air to see if that would help. Nothing was working though. We had to eventually go back to the house and let my mother know. I was really starting to panic to the point that I thought I was going to die.

It was pretty late at night when we got back to the house and woke up my mom. We let her know what was going on, but we never told her what we were doing, I just said that my heart was racing and pounding and that I thought there was something wrong with it. She told me to sit, calm down and breathe. Then she got me a paper bag to breathe in and out of.

After a while, there was a knock on the door. It was my uncle, my mother's brother.

"What is he doing here?" I asked.

We didn't have a car and my mom didn't drive, so she called him to take us to the hospital. We went to Harlem Hospital, where one of my aunts worked. She was on duty that night and had me admitted. They took me right in. Once you tell the hospital it's your heart, they usually don't have you wait. They did an EKG and all the other tests they do to rule out a heart attack. I remember clinching my chest and being curled up in a fetal position as I waited to hear the results of the tests.

My uncle, aunt and mother were over on the other side of the room talking. Suddenly, my uncle came over to me and bent down (he was a tall man) and asked me, "Do you smoke? Or have you had anything to smoke tonight?"

I was shocked when he asked me that. Out of all things he could say, why was he asking that?

At first, I said, "No," but eventually I did tell him. He went back over to where my mother and my aunt were and continued talking with them.

After a while, my mom came over, rubbed my head, and asked, "How are you feeling?"

I told her I was scared. "What is going on?" I asked.

"They don't know."

My uncle came back to me and he said, "I see this all the time working in corrections, when inmates smoke angel dust."

In my head, all I could think was, "Oh my!" His words took me back to my girlfriend's house earlier that evening, when I asked her, "What if they gave us some angel dust or put something in this weed?" The guy who purchased the weed for us lived in the second section of Bronxdale projects where we grew up. He was a cool guy, but that didn't mean Grandma hadn't done something. Still, I denied doing anything.

The doctor came in the room and spoke with my mother, uncle, and my aunt. I could hear a little bit of what they were saying. I do remember the doctor saying that everything looks good, that there was no need to be concerned with my heart. Then he walked over to me and asked, "Have you been going through stress? Or are there things that have been bothering you that you've been keeping in? Do you think that you might need to talk to someone?"

I looked at the doctor in disbelief. I wanted to ask, "What are you talking about man? What is going on with me?" I was still clutching my chest every time the pounding started back; my breath was short, and I was sweating profusely. The doctor told my mother that they were going to give me something to calm me down and that it was probably best that they keep me overnight for observation. I heard him use the word 'psychosomatic' when he was talking to my family. I didn't know what the word meant at the time, but I found out later that it was a physical illness or other condition caused or aggravated by a mental factor such as internal conflict or stress. In other words, it's when mental factors cause physical symptoms but there is no physical disease.

My mother, uncle and my aunt decided that me staying overnight was the best thing. I remember hearing the doctor say that they would take me to the psychiatric floor, and I would be watched there. They gave me an injection and my mom and uncle came over to me. They said goodnight and assured me they would be back in the morning to pick me up.

I begged my mom not to leave me.

"I want to go home. I don't want to go where there is crazy people." (That's what we called people with mental illnesses at the time. We know better now.)

Whatever they gave me started to kick in quick. I felt my body go real limp and heavy, and my speech slurred. I could barely move, but I remember my mom rubbing my forehead and saying, "I will be back in the morning."

I couldn't say anything though. I dozed off to sleep, and when I woke up, I was still feeling groggy and heavy. I opened my eyes to find a white man in a hospital gown bent over me, looking directly into my eyes, a smile on his face. I don't recall if I yelled at him to get out of my face; all I know is that I was terrified. He turned around and walked out of the room fast. I noticed then that I was not in the same place I was when I came into the hospital. I was in the psych ward. After a while, my mother walked in the room. Although I was glad that she was there to pick me up, I was harboring anger at her for leaving me there. How could a mother do that to her own child?

I don't recall any conversation we had until we were in the cab and on our way home. I was still feeling drugged up from whatever medication they gave me the night before.

When we were in the cab, my mom asked, "How are you feeling, are you okay?"

"How could you leave me there with a bunch of crazy people?" I told her about the man standing over me when I woke up. "What if he had done something to me, mommy? How would you have felt then?"

That was the guilt trip I tried to lay on her, but I was serious!

She apologized for leaving me there, but she said she didn't want to take me home and have something happen to me. She thought it was best to listen to the doctor and with my aunt working there, I would be okay.

Except my aunt didn't work in the psych ward where she could come and check on me from time to time. I told her as much, still terribly upset about the whole situation.

My mom mentioned to me that my uncle told her that I was smoking that night. I was mad at him after that. I had told him in confidence thinking he would not tell my mother, but I guess he felt like he couldn't hide that from his sister. I was so upset. At that moment, I felt like telling my mom some things about him that I knew that she didn't know. But my mom didn't seem angry. She just asked me, "Why did you smoke marijuana? Why did you feel the need to smoke and pick up another bad habit? You're already smoking cigarettes. I wish you would have never started."

I told her she didn't have to worry about me ever smoking weed again. I still didn't know if we had a bad bag of weed or if I smoked something else that triggered what occurred that night, but I wasn't going to do that again.

When we arrived home, I sat on the couch for a while. My mom sat down for a minute and let me know that the doctor gave her a referral to a psychiatrist and thought it might be a good idea for me to give it a try. She thought if I couldn't talk with her and let her know what was going on with me, maybe talking to someone else might be helpful.

I agreed to give it a try.

We went to the appointment at the scheduled time. The therapist introduced herself and told my mom that she was going to take me inside. When the session was done, she would bring me back out. I don't remember everything we talked about and how the conversation started. I believe I opened up about how hurt I was after my break-up with Antwon. I told her that it became hard for me after we parted ways because I would see him with different girls all the time. That was our first conversation.

I believe I went to her maybe two more times, but then I told my mother I didn't want to go back. Even though it felt good talking to someone about the things that I had been holding in for so long, she wasn't the one I wanted to continue conversing with. After my last visit with the therapist, I let her know that I would no longer continue with her services and that I would try to deal with things on my own, in my own way. I told her that I would learn to talk more about things and not hold them in to the point where it made me sick, and it would trigger panic and anxiety attacks. She prescribed an anti-depressant medicine for me, thinking it would help me, and that was the last of my therapy with her. I started taking the medication (I think it was called Xanax), but I didn't do well on it. I took it for about a week or two, but the side effects were horrible. One side effect that really stood out was the dry mouth: when I swallowed, my tongue stuck to the roof of my mouth. After that, I ended my relationship with that medication.

# Chapter 3

After what happened, I took the time to think about what I was going to do with the rest of my life. I started smoking more and more cigarettes, going in and out of depression and still trying to figure things out.

At that point, I decided that I wanted to act, model or sing. I started going to auditions for acting and for some modeling jobs, but I got discouraged in that area because my mother would tell me, "Girl, what are you going to do acting? You can't act." I remember one time she came with me to an audition for a test shoot for a modeling gig. It was for Faces International. They told me I did a great job, but there was one problem. I was a hairy young lady: I had a little mustache at the age of fifteen and wasn't very self-conscious about it. Well, the people at Faces International said I would have to get the hair removed that was over my lip.

"You mean shave?"

That was the end of that for me. I was not shaving or waxing my little bit of hair over my lip. So, we left, and I was no longer interested in going on any more auditions. But now I was self-conscious about my little mustache. Some people told me that it was cute and sexy, but in my head, I wondered if they would feel that way if they had it.

I don't know where the idea came from, but after that, I started writing a script for a television show. I called the show 'Friends!' This was way before the television show by the same name that everyone knows now. It was about me and my friends, Lia and Will. Thinking back on that now, I can't believe I wrote a whole script and never did anything with it. I did show it to my friends, but after that it went to the archives. It sat for many years and followed me wherever I went. I really didn't know what to do with it nor did I know anything about submitting it somewhere. I just did it for fun. It was something to keep my mind occupied.

"Yeah, it'll never make it. Just put it away in a folder somewhere," Will told me. And so, I did.

Then we saw the show 'Friends' come out. We couldn't believe it! We were shocked. Will told me, "Nik, you could have been rich!"

"Oh, but remember you said put the script up; it would never make it."

In the end, we just laughed about it. He was my best friend and we talked to one another like that. We are still friends forty years later.

After my ordeal with the panic attacks and auditioning for different projects. I still wasn't sure which direction my life was going in. Then one day, my mom asked me to go to the supermarket for her. On my way, I was stopped by a guy named Dwight.

"What's your name?" he asked me and proceeded to tell me that he lived right across the street in the Schyler building.

"It's nice to meet you," I responded, and told him my name. We became friends and talked for a while. I didn't think it would turn into anything serious because although he was a great guy, he absolutely was not my type. Dwight was dark-skinned, long, and lanky, and not attractive at all. But wouldn't you know it, we decided to make it official and became boyfriend and girlfriend.

Dwight admitted to me that he was talking with another young lady at the time. He said the girl was in love with him, that he was her first boyfriend, but now he was in love with me. He broke off things with her to be with me. I felt bad, because she and I were friends at the time, but Dwight insisted he wanted to be with me. We were together every day all day after that.

He was another one who was sexually active and sowing his seeds already. He never forced me into having sex with him. Dwight tried, but he was a gentleman and took his time and waited until I was ready. I don't know why but the last time he tried, I told him that I wanted to wait until my seventeenth birthday. He was okay with that, but that was mostly because it wasn't far away.

My seventeenth birthday came, and I was a nervous wreck, but I kept my word to Dwight, and he was my first.

He wasn't my type, but it was then that I started to fall in love with him. Long story short, my cycle didn't come the next month. I waited for it, but when it didn't come the second month, I went to the doctor and found out I was pregnant. I was in total shock. We weren't ready to be parents at seventeen.

I knew my mother would be so disappointed in me. I didn't want to tell her, but eventually I did, a whole month later. I didn't have the nerve to tell her right after I found out the news. I went in her room, told her that I needed to talk with her, and then just blurted out, "You're not going to be happy about what I am getting ready to tell you, but I am pregnant, Mom."

"What?" She said and put her head down in her hands. After a minute, she asked, "What do you want to do, Nikki?"

I told her that I wanted to keep the baby.

"Then we will get through this. It won't be easy, but we will make it work," she told me.

I was surprised. She did not chew my head off or yell at me when I told her, and that made me feel good.

When I was in my second trimester, I ran into Antwon. He just looked at me though and shook his head. "You gave me a hard time and you ended up getting pregnant by Dwight." Then he kept on walking. I was more hurt that he gave me the cold shoulder. I wasn't mad at him at all; if anything, I was saying the same thing inside. I was mad at myself for that!

I lost contact with Antwon. He moved upstate and I didn't speak to him for many years after that. I don't remember if I got the nerve up to ask for his phone number, or if I pulled up his business on the internet and found it that way. Either way, I reached out to him after many years, and he was so surprised to hear from me. He told me that he came back to New York to find me but heard that I moved out of state. I was a little disappointed, as feelings had started to come back after we conversed on the phone off and on, but things just weren't meant to be. However, we would remain friends for life.

I had a pretty good pregnancy: I didn't experience morning sickness and I only had cravings for pickles and potato chips. When I entered my second trimester, my baby started moving a lot. I was getting kicks all throughout the day and night. I told my mom that I thought the little one wanted to get out of my belly. I was convinced he might come early. But I got used to all the movement he would do and paid it no mind.

One evening, I went to the bathroom and could not stop urinating. My water had broken. I was home alone and scared. I don't know where everyone was. We didn't have cell phones then, so it was hard to reach one another if someone was out of the house. I ended up calling a close friend of the family who lived across the street and she took me to the hospital quickly. I was admitted and checked by the doctor. She told me I still had some fluid left and they wanted to keep the baby in as long as possible. To do that, they would have to put me in a position that was not going to be very comfortable for me.

Everyone came to the hospital and around nine hours later, I had the baby (I guess he was tired of staying in that position as well). Tyrell was born on November 23, 1987 at 7:13 a.m., weighing in at 2 pounds and 3 ounces. I could not hold him or lay him on my chest. They showed him to me quickly and then took him right over to the NICU (Neonatal Intensive Care Unit) because he was premature, and he could not breathe on his own. His organs, skin and lungs had barely developed, and he was so small.

After the nurse cleaned me up, she told me that the doctors would be in to talk with me as soon as they finished getting Tyrell hooked up and taken care of so that he had a fighting chance. All I could do was cry. Not knowing my baby would make it through the night was too much for me to handle. I stayed up all night worried.

I was able to go and see him the next day. When I got to the NICU and finally saw my baby with all those tubes hooked up to his little frail body, I teared up again. My heart was hurting for him. I had never seen a baby so small and fragile. It looked like he had no fat on his body at all, just bones. You could see every rib, and his little breaths were so deep. I was filled with all kinds of emotions at that very moment.

The Chief of the NICU came over and told me everything that was done and what every tube hooked up to him was for. My baby was fighting for his life, and I felt so helpless because there was nothing that I could do for him. I didn't want to leave his side. I stood right there and talked to him. I let him know that I would be there for him every single day, fighting with him.

As I was leaving the NICU, the doctor told me it was a critical time and they would watch him very closely, but they needed to be honest with me. There was a chance that he might not make it through the night, but he was getting the best care possible to give him every fighting chance. They also told me that I was welcome to come any time that I wanted; and if my baby did make it, he could be in the hospital for months. That was the start of my talking to God, with me asking him, "Please let my baby live."

When it was time for me to leave the hospital, I was filled with such sadness. I didn't want to leave my son. I was able to touch his little, fragile hand, and let him know that I would be at that hospital every day until he was released to come home. I also told him, "Thank you for fighting to live." I cannot explain it, but in that moment, it felt like there was a bright light that was shining on his chest. Not the light from the heated lamp that was over him, but like a light that was shining through the window on him. It was so bright, but it wasn't even sunny out that day. It was unusual and amazing. A peace just came over me and I just felt like everything was going to be alright. I was able to leave without my heart feeling heavy the way it felt before I entered the unit. I believe that was God letting me know Tyrell would be okay. He was going to be my miracle baby.

I was at that hospital every day. The hospital was not a hop skip and a jump from my house; it was quite far actually, but I made it there. I took the train, I took cabs, I did what I had to do to go see my son. I didn't care, I just needed to be there for him. He struggled a lot with breathing on his own. Then he developed other health issues that affect premature babies. I hated having to see my baby get blood work done. It was extremely hard for them to find veins because he was so tiny.

In the second week of his hospital stay, I arrived for my visit and went upstairs to see Tyrell like usual. When I got to the NICU, I noticed that his nails were a little blue. I spoke to the head nurse and asked her what was going on with him.

"It's from the arterial sticks. The veins blow every time they try to get an IV started. It seems that circulation is not good."

"What are you saying?" I demanded.

The Chief Surgeon came over to talk with me and said, "This sometimes happens with preemie babies. It is hard to find veins and sometimes they blow from medications that have to be given or bloodwork that has to be done." He told me so that they wouldn't have to keep sticking him, they were going to have to put an IV into his vein in the neck.

I was so heartbroken. I found myself talking to God more than I ever had. I just started asking Him to help my son, to strengthen him, to help him fight. There was just so much going on. My son was also laying under a bright light because he was suffering with jaundice. I was feeling down knowing that he was suffering with all these different things in his fragile little body.

As the days went on, I noticed that my son's fingers (along with his fingernails) were turning bluer. The doctor told me that he was having problems with circulation to his hand and that they believed gangrene (death of tissue) was setting in. My heart was in my stomach. I could not believe that this was happening to my little baby. My son ended up losing his five digits (fingers) on his left hand. Tissue died and there was no blood circulation going to his fingers. They shriveled up and looked like raisins, and as time went on, eventually they fell off. He didn't even need surgery to remove them. The doctors and nurses put medication on his hand to keep it clean and bandaged it up to prevent infection.

This was something I could not wrap my head around. I was lost. I kept saying, "Why God? Why did this have to happen to my baby?"

Tyrell remained in the hospital for around five months until he was able to go home. I kept my promise to him and visited with him every single day for those five months. Tyrell was a strong little baby; he had problems breathing and had to go back and forth on the ventilator, but he fought. He got better and stronger, gained weight, and was eventually released to go home.

What a bittersweet moment that was. I was so happy to hear the doctor say that Tyrell should be able to leave the following week. When that time came, I went to pick my baby up and we left that hospital for good. I was ecstatic the whole day, I was smiling, my heart was singing, and I felt complete now.

As the days went on, I started to learn about motherhood and raising a child. I felt myself having moments of sadness and I started slipping into depression. My thoughts were all over the place. I started worrying and asking God, "How will I be able to take care of a child with a handicap? How will my child feel once he gets older and goes to school?" I was fine while he was in his infancy, but when he started growing and learning to crawl, and touching things, I found myself overloading my brain with thoughts of pity. "Why Tyrell, God? Why me? I had plans; I didn't sign up for this kind of hurt."

I tried at this time to get close to God, but I felt so far from Him. I even picked up smoking cigarettes again. I was thankful though to have my mom there with me. She was such a help and loved her first grandchild with everything in her. She would make sure I got up early in the mornings and took Tyrell out for walks to get that fresh morning air. I think she noticed that I was sinking into depression. I tried to work part-time to keep my mind stayed on other things rather than thinking about how hard life was going to be for us. I worked as long as I could, but with everything going on, it was hard to hold on to a job.

When Tyrell turned two years old, he began therapy to learn how to navigate life using one hand. We had appointments two to three times a week, along with other appointments that he had for developmental delays. My life was put on hold and every moment was focused on Tyrell for the first several years of his life. The older he got, the more difficult things became trying to teach him how to live with one hand. Anxiety and panic attacks began to happen to me once again. But I had help from my mother, Dwight, and Dwight's mom to get me through that. They gave me time to rest and gather my thoughts as I was trying to cope with these panic attacks. We spent a lot of time at Dwight's mom's house. She lived right down the block from where we stayed, which was very convenient.

There wasn't much to do living in the projects so I would take my son outside to play with Zelma's son. They grew up together and became close. I would go to church sometimes just like I used to before I had Tyrell, but that was basically it. We would go outside and let them play in the back of the building at the little park that was there. I was so very overprotective of Tyrell when it came to him playing and hurting himself, but Zelma would say, "Let that boy play and fall and be a boy." I used to get so mad at that. I didn't want my baby getting hurt. No one could understand how I felt. I wanted to protect him. I didn't want him to suffer through any more unnecessary hurt and pain like what he had to experience when he was a baby.

# Part 2

# Making Life-Changing Decisions and Living in Regret

# Chapter 4

Dwight and I stayed together for around two more years. He began cheating on me, hanging out all times of the night and doing drugs. I couldn't deal with it anymore, so we broke up. This was a hard break-up for me as well. I was in a deep dark space and was having panic and anxiety attacks that lasted up to a week at a time. I had to re-evaluate some things.

I moved out and got my own apartment but was over at my mother's house every day. That's where Tyrell's friend was and who he played with all the time. But then Zelma and her mom told me that they were moving south. I was devastated. Our sons were inseparable. Her son was my godson. But now Tyrell would be losing his best friend and wouldn't have him to play with anymore. What in the world was I going to do now?

Zelma and her family moved down to North Carolina and left us. I decided to visit them one summer. We stayed for a week or two. I loved it. Tyrell and his god-brother were so happy to see one another. I really didn't want to leave when it was time to go. It was so clean down there—what a change from New York!

When we drove back home, it was back to life as usual. I started doing a lot of thinking about my life and my son's life. I met someone else, Dee, and started seeing him. Eventually I allowed him to move in with me. I don't know why I did that. Dee was not good for me at all; he was a drug dealer and had anger issues; and he didn't like Dwight. When he would see him, he would look at him with so much hate, and call him derogatory names. I don't know where the hate came from, but this was one of the worst mistakes of my life. I asked him to leave after a while and discovered it was extremely hard to get him out of my house.

Then I found out that Dee was talking to a girl who lived up the street from my apartment building. She called his phone one time and I answered. I asked who she was, and she said she was talking to Dee. When I told him that I answered his phone, he became so angry and started cussing. He insisted she was just a friend and that there was nothing going on. She was only calling for some earphones that he had borrowed from her.

But Dee was sneaking around with her. I remember looking out my window the next day and seeing his car pass the building and go up the street to a private house. I knew that was his car because of a distinctive dent it had on the side. I said nothing though. I got in the bed and went to sleep. I called the girl the next day (I had written down her number when she called initially) and asked her if she lived up the block in a private house. She said she did and then confirmed that Dee had visited her.

That was all I needed to know. The day after that, I asked Dee if that was his car up the street going to a private house and is that where the girl lived. He admitted it and said he went to give her the earphones back and that he would cut the friendship off. I tried to break up with him and he begged me to stay with him, promising never to see her again, even though there was nothing going on. You know I didn't believe that, but I took him back anyway. Dee was so very wrong for me. I don't know why I had a thing for bad boys. Then to make matters worse, I found out he was a drug dealer. I really wanted out of the relationship now.

One day, I went around my mother's neighborhood to visit. Dee came around the way and I was standing near a car talking to him when my neighbor came out the building. He had some words with him—Dee had had a fling with his girlfriend. She was also my friend and I knew she had a little fling with Dee before I got with him. It wasn't serious because she loved her boyfriend very much. I guess it was something that just happened during their brief break up but that caused problems in our friendship. Anyway, my neighbor pulled out a gun and was aiming it towards the car and saying something. Then Dee pulled out his gun and I don't remember what I did, all I know is that gunfire erupted. I could not believe that I was in the middle of a shoot-out with them. I really can't remember if I ducked down or ran away. I know one thing: I was terrified!

My neighbor and I didn't talk for a really long time. I was hurt by all that occurred. I saw my mother looking out of the window, along with all our other neighbors, when the gunfire started. I don't think she knew who it was, but she did know my boyfriend and she wasn't too happy with my choice of men. She remembered his car from when I allowed him to meet her, and she asked if that was him. I told her yes and explained what happened. She really was not happy with me after that. I wasn't happy with myself. I was trying to get away and out of this relationship. I went home and started thinking about going down south for a visit to get away.

Tyrell and I went to visit Zelma and her son for a week again. When we got back home, I was just sick of looking at this man in my house. Tyrell asked me a day or two later after we came back from North Carolina, "Can we move down there?"

I thought long and hard about it and since I wasn't happy in my present predicament, I knew this might be my way out of this relationship. I knew Dee wouldn't leave this drug life that he established in New York. That was his whole life, that's all he knew. This was my opportunity to get away from this nut. He was too jealous and possessive of me. I never really told my family how he was. They were already upset that I was with him; I didn't want to make it worse.

I told my mom that I was going to move down south. She didn't want me to be so far away, but she supported my decision and said it was up to me. Thinking back on everything that we had been through in the first eight years of Tyrell's life—all the depression, appointments, ear surgery (my son suffered with ear infections often), and therapy, I was ready for a new start, for me and especially a better life for my son.

A few days later, I told Dee that I decided to move to North Carolina. I never saw him quiet in my life. He was shocked and asked, "Where is all this coming from?" He left the house for a while, came back around an hour later, huffing and puffing!

"How are you just going to spring that on me, that you're moving down south. What about us? That's it for us?"

In my head, I was thinking, "Yes! That is it for us!" I was ready to start building a new life without a bunch of mess in it, but I didn't tell him that.

We remained together for the next six months. During this time, Dee was being nice to me, talking about what he would do to help me. He would drive with me when I went house hunting. We would stay with Zelma and her man while we were there looking. I would be with her and he would hang with him.

When it was time to go, I remember him telling me, "I can't be down there. It's too slow and these n****'s ain't about nothing!"

I was so happy to hear that!

Dee came with me one more time. I found a house the second time I went down south. When I first walked into the home, I told him I was not going to cover the back windows or door, I wanted natural light coming in.

He said, "You're crazy! You gonna live here with all these windows and a glass door in the back and you're not going to put curtains up?"

I had said that for a reason: I didn't want him to get any ideas about coming with me.

We drove back to New York the next day. I settled down, relaxed, and gathered my thoughts. I was a little nervous that I was about to make a big move away from all my family. I started wondering if we would be lonely without them. Why was I taking my son away from his grandmother who he loved so much and she him? I had to tell myself, "Nikki, you are doing the right thing. You will be able to go back home and visit your family and they will be able to come and visit you."

I don't know if I was having second thoughts, or I was just a little nervous to know that I would be on my own without the help of my mom. But it was time to grow up and make a new start for my little family. I had to tell myself, "You can do it! This is the best thing."

I started to feel better the next day and got my important paperwork together so that I could head back down south in a few weeks. I took my mom and stepfather down with me when I did the closing on the house. My mom told me how beautiful the home was, though she thought it might be too much house for just me. It was three thousand square feet, with four bedrooms and three full baths. I was the first owner: it was newly built in a new subdivision that only had two other homes in it at the time. I was so happy that I was going to be able to raise my son there and give him the freedom to go outside of his own house and play in his backyard. It was what I wanted for him. He was so happy, running around the house, showing my mom his room. It made my heart smile. Everything was done: we closed on the house, headed back to New York the next day, and I started packing up the apartment to get ready to move out of New York City and start our new life. I was so excited, I packed up just about the whole apartment the next day.

Dee came by and said he was going to help me pack. But I had already done everything. I didn't have boxes taped up yet, and I saw him looking in the boxes to see what was in them.

I asked him, "Why do you keep looking through the boxes?"

"I'm just seeing what you have in them. What's the problem?"

I shut my mouth so I wouldn't start an argument. Any little thing I said ticked him off at that moment.

"So, you really leaving me?" Dee asked.

"I have to go," I told him. I don't know why I said it, but I knew for sure he wouldn't do it. I said, "Yeah, I'm going, you could come if you want."

"You know, I can't go! I have too much going on here."

I was relieved and thanked God!

# Chapter 5

It was moving day! I was excited, scared, and nervous all at the same time. Tyrell was all smiles and ready to go! What could you expect though? He was a child and excited to move to where his friend was, whom he missed so dearly.

Dee called and told me he would be over in a little while to see me off. When he arrived, I was in the process of putting things in the boxes and taping them up. As I began to head to Tyrell's room and gather up some of his things, he came behind me and said, "I been thinking. I think I'm gonna go and get out of here."

My heart dropped. I said, "What are you talking about?"

"How you mean?" He was Jamaican, so, 'how you mean?' meant 'what are you talking about?'

My whole day was messed up. Excitement turned into anger.

He said, "You said the other day I can come if I want."

I was so angry I could have punched myself in the mouth.

Dee said, "So what is the problem?"

I had to be straight up with him and tell him that I did not want that, "I don't need you down there with me. I'm trying to leave this New York life behind. You are a drug dealer, and I don't want that nowhere around us."

Oh, Dee was not happy. He was mad. He started pacing the floor, going back and forth, nostrils flaring out. He raised his voice and said, "So you were just talking? You were playing games?"

"Things are not the best between us," I said, "I told you I don't want your lifestyle around us."

He started pleading and said he wouldn't do that. He wanted to make a new life for himself too. He would find a job and get out of that life. All he wanted to do was be with me.

I put my foot in my mouth and said three words that would set off three years of turmoil: "You can come." I was so angry with myself. But what I didn't know is that it would start me on my journey to Christ.

I settled into my new home. Everything was good in the beginning. I found a job, started going to church off and on with my girlfriend and her mother, trying to get closer to the Lord. Dee would get up in the morning and tell me he was going job hunting. This went on for months, but he was lying! Dee wasn't looking for a job. He was getting to know the area and the people who could help him start his drug dealing down here. He became cool with

Zelma's man, until he started meeting other people over in their apartment complex. The hanging out, drinking and smoking weed began and became an all-day everyday exercise. He didn't have a car at the time, so he would have me take him where he needed to go or he would take my car, which I absolutely did not want because he did not have a license.

Things started getting bad for me. Dee would have me drop him off at my girlfriend's complex. I would go inside to see her for a little while then leave. He would call me in the wee hours of the morning to get him. Zelma noticed how stressed I was becoming, even fearful. He started drinking a lot, smoking, and arguing with me for no reason. He was just a nasty person. Everything changed about him when we came to North Carolina. The alcohol and the weed, and him having to look over his shoulder every waking minute made the evil in him really come out.

I found myself going to church and talking to God a little more. But it didn't seem like God was hearing me, so I eased up. I was so stressed out and not in my right mind. I just wanted Dee to go. He would come home drunk sometimes and wake me out of my sleep to get him something to eat. I had to get up in the morning for work, but he didn't care, he was wasted. The first year was the beginning of hell on earth for me. It was almost the end of 1997. Dee asked me if I could put a car in his name so that he did not have to bother me to take him anywhere or pick him up from somewhere or use my car since I always made such a big deal when he had it.

"No, I am not putting any car in your name, sorry," I told Dee.

He was not happy at all.

"What is the big deal?" he said.

"What's the big deal? Really, you're asking me that?"

He left the room and went downstairs. I went to sleep.

The next day, he asked, "What about a motorcycle?"

I agreed to the motorcycle but let him know that I was getting it for me and that he could use it. I always wanted one, but I also did not want him driving my car anymore. I got the bike, but I don't think I had it more than two to three months before it was stolen or wrecked, I don't remember. I was going through so much at the time, I was always stressed out. The panic and anxiety attacks started back. I had lost a lot of weight. I could barely eat, let alone focus. Dee started fussing outside of my job because I didn't want him taking my car, and I would give it to him so that I didn't get in trouble or fired. I would go to work miserable; he would pop up at my job, get my car and pick me up when I got off.

Zelma saw what was happening and asked me, "Are you scared of him?"

I don't remember what I told her, but the truth was, yes. The verbal and emotional abuse had been so bad that I was scared of him. He always tried to intimidate me. I would argue with him and yell too, but I knew to calm down when I saw him looking at me like he was about to do something. As nasty as he was, he never hit me. I knew of a couple of girls in New York that he put his hands on and I just prayed he would not touch me.

I didn't want to act too scared though, so I had to pretend like I wasn't. Dee would tell me, "You're the only girl that don't act like a b****. Maybe that's why I love you and stay with you. Had it been anybody else, I would've cuffed them by now. You give me a run for my money."

One time, we went to New York to visit family and stopped by Dee's parents' home. He argued and talked to them with no respect, even though they were the sweetest people in the world. I remember thinking, "Wow! If he talks to them like that, he doesn't care about how he talks to nobody! He has some screws loose." I didn't know where all this built-up anger came from inside of him, but he was not wrapped too tight.

His mom and I became very close, and she told me that he changed when he started hanging in the streets. He was an intelligent, well-mannered child when he was younger, but the streets and jail made him into the man he was.

I remember visiting their house another time and praying that being in New York would make him miss it and he would want to stay. But he came back with me. On the ride home, I did a lot of thinking. Number one, I was getting back to church as soon as Sunday came around. I needed to get closer to the Lord. I needed help and I needed direction.

Sunday came. Dee wasn't at the house; he had stayed out all night. I got up, showered, and got myself ready for church. I went to Zelma's house to pick her up and saw him coming over to the car as I was getting out of it. I don't know where he stayed or came from, but he sure spotted my car.

"What are you doing?" he asked.

"I'm going to church!" I told him.

"Oh yeah?" He grabbed my pantyhose/stockings (the kind that had a seam running up the back of the leg) and ripped my whole left side. "You not going nowhere with those on." Dee was a jealous, insecure, possessive person who would see me in sweats all day if it were up to him. He would argue with me when I washed my hair and blowed it out nice and straight, because I looked too good.

Zelma saw what happened and she asked me if I was coming in. I told her that I was going home to change. She knew what was up though. I'd call her from time-to-time and confide in her. I would let her know some of the things that I was experiencing. She was concerned with me being down here with him, but I would tell her, "Don't worry, it's going to be okay."
I know she wanted to say something so bad, but she didn't.

He got in the car, I left Zelma's complex and went home. I didn't even want to go to church after that. I was so mad, I wanted to punch him in the face.

A week after all this happened, Dee was over in the complex and Zelma called me and told me, "He just shot up this house a few doors from mine." I was just too through. I prayed and prayed that he would leave. I didn't want no trouble. I was sure people thought he was with me. He used to drive my car all the time. What if someone did something to me to get back at him? I had a child that I had to protect and care for.

It got to the point that whenever I heard the garage door, my heart would start racing, because I never knew where Dee's mind was and if he was going to start with me. He would come in, wake me out of my sleep, and just begin unnecessary arguments with me. He told me a couple of days later not to go over to my friend's house because he got into an altercation with some people over there. He said, "I shot up the house because they said they was going to call the cops on me."

That was one thing Dee used to always stress: that he better not ever hear nobody say that they were going to call the cops on him. If you said the word 'cop', his whole facial expressions change; he would look crazy, and his nostrils would flare up. It used to scare me and make me think twice about calling the police. I remember he used to say that it wouldn't take but one phone call from jail if anybody ever called the cops on him.

By this time, I was really sick of him and struggling with the fact that I allowed him to come down here to North Carolina with me. I would always beat myself up. My mind was all over the place, thinking about how to get this man out of my house. Dee had already made a life for himself there. He started cheating, staying out all night, sometimes two days in a row. He met someone (she was a customer of his) and stayed at her house and did his dealings from there. That's also the place he would bring his other girls he was cheating with. He hated the fact that I would go to Zelma's house, because he knew I would find out what he was doing if I was out, and he didn't like that. He wanted me to stay in the house and that was it.

I didn't move to North Carolina to stay inside though, so I had to deal with the arguments all the time. My godson was the only person that Tyrell had to play with, and I wasn't going to let Dee make my son miserable. I put up with his nasty attitude and being mad because I was over there. Zelma and her man knew what was going on, and she tried in so many ways to let me know indirectly. They felt bad for me and what I was going through, but what could they do?

I was over Zelma's house soon afterward and we were outside. There were a couple of girls walking by, and Zelma told me that Dee was talking to one of the young ladies. I could only shake my head. They were teenage girls. Dee was messing with babies! I was often told that southern girls had a thing for New York bad boys. It seemed to be true because they didn't care if he was with somebody or not. I eventually confronted the girl and Dee, blowing his cover. But he became angrier and more verbally and emotionally abusive from there on.

# Chapter 6

One morning, I woke up, did my usual routine of getting my son up and getting him ready for school. I noticed though that he didn't seem very happy. I asked him, "What's wrong?"

Tyrell said, "I don't want to go to school."

He was finally feeling down about his hand and how the kids in his school stared at him. That was something I was anticipating; I just didn't know when it would affect him. Well, this was the time. I could do nothing but hug him at that very moment and let him know that everything was going to be alright. I had to explain to him what I didn't even understand: that he should not worry about the stares. Some people don't mean to stare, I told him, they were just looking and wondering what happened to his hand.

I was mad as I was telling Tyrell this though. All I could do was think back to when the stares were coming at me as I walked down the streets in New York. I held a lot of anger inside me because of that. When people would stare (kids and adults), it would take everything in me not to say something. I had to really pray and ask God to help me with that.

I also had to pray hard for my baby boy, who was now experiencing the very same thing. It was hard to deal with a child who had a handicap and was teased by his peers in school. It was a very dark moment for both of us. All I could do was give it to God. I also had to talk to my son daily and reassure him that this would eventually stop. People would not stare at him forever, because they would get used to seeing him every day. "You will even make friends," I told him.

He told me that nobody wanted to be friends with him because of his hand.

I had to interject and let him know that was not the reason. "God will send you a friend, just wait and see!"

I found myself carrying more than I could bear. Depression crept in, and anxiety and panic attacks started happening more frequently. I started smoking more and more cigarettes, up to a pack a day. I felt like I couldn't handle things anymore. I needed help. Something clicked inside my head and I thought of my brother, Howie. He was still in New York at the time. Something said, "Ask him to move down here and stay with you." I did. I just knew if Howie came down, Dee would leave. I don't think he even hesitated.

The next day, I got a call from my cousin, Clay.

"Can I come down too?" he asked.

That sounded like music to my ears! I said, "Sure!" and imagined how Dee was about to pack up his stuff and get out of here. Surely, he was not going to want to stay with Howie and Clay! That night, I let him know that my brother and cousin were coming down to live with us.

Oh, if the devil had horns, you would have seen them on him that night.

"WHAT?" Dee yelled, and I mean loud.

Tyrell came out of his room and asked, "What was that?"

That's how loud Dee yelled. I told my son it was nothing, and he went back upstairs.

"What are you saying to me?" Dee asked. I repeated myself, and he went off. He said, "You think I want to be around here with a bunch of n****'s? I did that in jail, I'm not trying to do it again."

I said, "Well, I don't know what to tell you, but they will be coming down. My family would feel much better if I had relatives down here."

"Feel better about what?" he yelled. "You telling your family I'm doing something to you or something?"

There was nothing but cussing after that. He picked up his gun, paced the floor and left the house.

Howie was excited to come down. He thought he would be chilling with Dee, whom he considered a cool dude, but he didn't know how he was treating his sister. It would have been a different story and they probably wouldn't have gotten along out the gate. Howie was very protective of me and so were the male cousins in my family.

When I first got with Dwight, my little brother was not happy, nor was he having it. He followed me down the street when I went to his house and he waited outside of his building for me. I told Howie to go on home now and boy was he angry. There was a chair right outside the building; next thing we heard was a big crash. Howie threw that chair into the lobby window and was yelling at Dwight to leave his sister alone. I could not believe it. I told him to take his tail home!

In any case, things started getting bad with Dee after I broke the news to him about my brother and cousin coming down. He became even more verbally and mentally abusive. He continued trying to intimidate me, especially since Howie and Clay weren't going to be down for another month or two.

I decided to get a seasonal job for the holidays since they were approaching. I had never worked two jobs, but I did everything I could to stay away from Dee. My neighbor was willing to let Tyrell go over to her house until I got home. I went to Dillard's department store and left with my part time job. I informed Dee that I found a job for the holidays. He didn't mind. I went to Dillard's the next week to start working. On my first day, they put me in the men's suit department. I had a good first day. I believe they had me on the schedule three days in a row. I went to work the second day. I was straightening up my area where the men's shirts were and who pops up? I never told Dee the department I worked in—he must have walked around the whole store until he found me.

"What are you doing?" Dee demanded. His face was all screwed up.

I said, "Working, what are you talking about? And what are you doing here?"

He started getting loud. "What are you doing here? Why are you working over here?" He meant in the men's department.

"Because this is the department they put me in."

"You need to tell them to change you before I break your face!"

My nerves were torn to pieces, knowing this was going to be a big thing later. I had Tyrell stay at his friend's house that night. When I got home, I showered and got in the bed. It might have been three o'clock in the morning when I heard the garage door. My heart started racing, I pretended like I was sleeping. Dee came right upstairs, poked me hard and said, "Get up!"

I said, "What happened?"

"Get up!" Dee yelled. "Come here!" He was in the hallway now.

"What?" I asked.

He dangled keys in my face.

"What the hell are these?" he asked.

I said, "Keys, and what?" I knew nothing about them and knew he was just trying to set me up.

"Whose keys are these? I found them in your car."

"Man, you didn't find no keys in my car, so why you're trying to start something, I don't know," I said, and tried to walk away. But he pulled me back and started poking me on my forehead!

"Who you had in the car?" he asked.

I started getting mad because Dee kept telling me I was messing around. He was wasted and mad from earlier and trying to pick a fight. I left and went to bed. He followed and went right to sleep.

An hour later, I heard him get up. I thought he might have been going to use the bathroom and he did, just not the room that had the toilet in it. He was urinating in the corner of the room. I started screaming, "What are you doing? You are urinating in the room. You're not in the bathroom!"

Dee slurred his words. "I'm using the bathroom," he said and finished. I went to bed and cried.

I had to work at Dillard's the next afternoon. It was the weekend, around 12:00pm, when I was getting ready for work. I gathered my pocketbook and keys, but he stopped me and asked, "Where are you going?"

"Work."

"I know you don't think you going back to that job in the men's department," he said.

"Yes, I am! What is wrong with working in the men's department?"

"Go on and try it. I'm gonna break every cussing window on your car!" He had a blade in his hand too. He was going to slash every tire if I got in the car to go to Dillard's. I was furious. I didn't have the energy to deal with him, so I didn't go back to that job.

This was the type of turmoil I was going through with this lunatic. A young man said hello to us one morning when he came into the Waffle House where we were eating breakfast. I said good morning, but Dee said nothing. His nostrils flared up, and I knew he was going to have something to say about me speaking to the young fellow. It's not like he was just talking to me, but that's just how nasty of a person Dee was. But I wasn't that kind of person. People would speak and he'd say nothing, but I spoke to people and smiled all the time. A big argument ensued after we got in the car. He got in the back seat and said, "Don't you ever talk to no n**** while you're with me. You not gonna disrespect me like that."

I yelled back at Dee and told him that the young man said good morning to both of us. "Why are you so hateful and nasty? Don't you ever call me that again. I have never called you out your name so don't do it to me."

He had a comb in his hand, and he moved up behind me and glided it across my neck as if it was a blade.

I screamed, "Are you crazy! Don't put your hand on me."

Dee slapped me on the side of my face from behind. I was in total shock and said nothing else. He had never touched me before and that was the last straw. I couldn't wait for my family to come down. But I also knew things could and would get worse after that.

I continued to confide in Zelma. She was concerned with me down here with him. But I would tell her, "Don't worry, it's going to be okay."

My mind was all over the place now, not thinking great things. I started sleeping with a knife under my pillow wondering if I should kill him that night. I wrestled with this for an exceptionally long time. I couldn't wait for Sunday so that I could go to church and get my mind off all these bad thoughts I was having. I don't think anyone can understand how a woman gets trapped in a relationship unless you have been there. I was one of those who called women stupid for staying in abusive relationships. Now I can totally understand how a woman could feel stuck. No matter how many times I told Dee to please leave, to find his own place, he'd come back and say, "I ain't going nowhere! I'm not doing nothing to you. You talk like a n**** and then when I step to you like one, you blame me."

Don't ever let a man blame you for his wrongdoing, because they will.

My spirit and mental being was so exhausted with what I was going through. I tried my best to keep it from my son Tyrell, and I think I did a good job with that, but I got to the point where I called my older cousins in New York and asked them if they could do me a favor and kill somebody for me?

They said, "What's going on? You know we will, but the thing is, will you be able to live with it? That is something that may play in your mind and you can't shake it."

I had to think about Tyrell, that's why I didn't do it. Every night I would be shaking because I wanted to kill Dee while he was asleep, but the thought of leaving my son behind messed me up. That's why I figured if somebody else did it I might be okay. I really needed God. This wasn't the kind of person I was, to talk about killing somebody. And because of where I was mentally, it was imperative that I seek God even more. I didn't want to think the way I was thinking. I didn't want to lay in my bed each night plotting and planning. That was just not me.

I started going to church more, getting closer to the Lord, building my relationship with Him, and allowing myself to get still so that I could hear His voice. I was enjoying every moment of it. But I was still smoking cigarettes. I felt bad and was self-conscious about it because I would smoke in the car on the way to church and try my best to get the smell off my fingers and hope that it wasn't strong in my clothes. It took me a good while to give up the cigarettes; after all, the smoking calmed me down with all that I was dealing with.

I couldn't wait for Wednesdays and Sundays to come around. Bible Study and Sunday Service were my safe, sane places. I felt like I had no worries or cares in the world when I was there. They were my refuge and present help in times of trouble. I would be around people who would pray for me and lift my spirits. As I was learning God, it was good to be around people who already knew Him and had a relationship with Him. It was encouraging for me to see that because it made me want to know God in a greater way as well.

I was already fascinated when people would get the Holy Ghost. I wanted so bad for that to happen for me. I wanted to know what it felt like. It was one of the reasons I kept going to church: I went with expectation, waiting for the Holy Ghost to hit me. Sunday after Sunday, nothing happened. All I got was the word. What God was saying was all I needed right then. I had to keep telling myself, the Holy Ghost will come.

I can remember I was in church one day testifying about how good God was and how He was protecting me and keeping me, when, suddenly, my hand went up and my throat got hot. All I could do was stop talking and put my hand up and say, "Thank you Jesus." It was like fire that came in my throat. It was such an overwhelming feeling, but I felt so different after and closer to God.

# Part 3

# Adding Fuel
# to The Fire

Monique Headecker-Green

# Chapter 7

I was so excited when the time came for my brother and my cousin to move down. I wasn't going to let anything, or anybody ruin my day of happiness. Tyrell was excited as well. Clay didn't come down the same time Howie did, he moved two to three months later. When Howie arrived, we sat down and talked about what I expected from him and what I didn't want to see. Howie wasn't a saint by a long shot, but he was definitely a great, well-mannered, and respectful guy. Our mom raised us on her own, but she instilled great morals and values into all her children. Now I will say, he was spoiled, being the youngest and a boy at that! But I can't even explain the love that I always had for Howie. I was overprotective of him, just like he was my son. If someone did something to Howie, I wanted to hurt them. I wondered over the things I would think of to hurt them back and that is when I came to realize that we are all capable of doing something bad. If you messed with my family, it didn't take much for me to start thinking crazy thoughts that I shouldn't.

Howie said he would find a job and do the right thing. He never held onto a job long at all. He probably only had two in his life that I can remember. He was too busy making money in the streets and you know once they get a taste of making that fast money, it's hard to let it go and make money the legit way.

Howie eventually found a job at CarMax, but he didn't have transportation, so I had to take him to work. Things were okay in the household for a while. Howie would go with Dee sometimes to the apartment complex where Zelma lived, and where he did his mess. After a while, all that changed. Howie would get dressed thinking he was going to hang out and catch a ride with Dee so he could go with him around the neighborhood and hang out with my girlfriend's man. I guess he was trying to get to know people there since this was where he was going to be residing. I really didn't want my brother over there, but I couldn't keep him in the house. He was grown.

One day, Dee was leaving out the door, and I told him, "Howie is getting dressed, I guess he wants to catch a ride and go with you over there."

That was the start of him acting funny.

"I'm not waiting for him," he said. "He's not coming down here to hang out with me, you take him. Your brother talks too much and is too trusting, can't do it."

This was just an excuse though. He didn't want to do it.

Howie came downstairs ready to go and asked where Dee was.

"He left," I said and told him the things he said. Things were never the same between them again.

I continued to take Howie to work and drop him off around Zelma's way whenever he wanted to go. Eventually my mother took a load off me and purchased a car for Howie so that he could get around. That was a big relief for me, and I was grateful for that. Afterward, my brother was able to get around and go where he pleased at any time he wanted.

But tension started building in my household. Dee would come in sometimes or walk around the house and barely speak. The truth was he was mad.

"I'm down here," Howie told me, "I can now go where I want to and I'm getting to know people that he might know, and he knows that I will start hearing about what he's doing out here and with who."

Clay eventually moved down too. He got settled in and found a job at the Home Depot not far from the house. Howie took him to work, or he drove the car there when Howie didn't need to use it. But with all of them in the house, it was just getting more and more difficult to deal with Dee's nasty attitude. He came in one night, woke me up, and with his gun in his hand, said, "Yo, go tell him to move his car."

"What?"

"Go and tell him to move his car," Dee repeated. "I can't get in the garage because he is blocking the door." He was pacing back and forth, breathing hard, his nostrils flared.

I got up, went downstairs, and saw the light on in the front sitting area. Howie was up.

"Can you move your car so this creep could pull his car in?"

My brother was not happy.

"What? Why are you coming down here telling me?"

"Can you just move it? I don't want you two getting into it, especially here."

I don't know if Howie did it on purpose or not, but he was muttering something and cursing as he was walking away. I wanted to pick something up and hit him over the head and knock him out, that's how mad I was, but I prayed instead, "Lord, please don't let there be no fight in here tonight." I hated myself for always giving in and doing what Dee asked me, or on most occasions, told me to do.

I don't know where Clay was that night, but he never really knew Dee. He met him once in New York, but never really knew him like that; and when he moved down to North Carolina, he didn't really speak to him or see him much. I was dealing with three grown men, walking around the house, and not talking to one another! I'm sure they would have loved to go at it. That's how much anger I'm sure Dee was holding in because my brother was there. Likewise, Howie was holding things in because I asked him not to say anything to him. I knew my brother didn't have a gun on him (none that I knew of), and I knew Dee did and was known to have used it. He was actually sleeping with it under his pillow since my brother and cousin moved in!

Can you imagine living like this? It wasn't a good feeling. I can't explain the level of stress and weight I was carrying. It was too much for a person to carry, but during that, my walk with Christ became stronger. Because of everything that I was dealing with, church became my safe place. I decided then to give my life to Christ. I had gone to church and prayed before, but I was still trying to run my own life, and let me tell you, I was failing. I was smoking a pack of cigarettes a day from the stress, verbal, mental and now physical abuse. I found myself one night opening my second pack of cigarettes, and I knew then I had to do something. If the stress didn't kill me, surely the smoking would. I tried to stop smoking on my own many occasions, but I wasn't successful at it. I was too addicted to the nicotine.

Now, even though I hadn't surrendered my life completely to Christ at this point, I can say that my spirit was becoming sensitive to what God was speaking to me and telling me what to do. I marveled to the point where I said, "Wow, God, I can't believe that You're speaking to me and You are using me to bless people." One time, God had me stop at a store and grab a couple of items. I didn't know why He was telling me to do this, but I did it, then got back in my car and drove off. As I was driving home, I saw a young lady on the divider that separated the road. I saw her and thought she was either homeless or in need of transportation. I wanted so bad to ask if she needed a ride, but I kept going. As I did, God said, "Turn back around and give her that bag of snacks you just purchased."

"What did you say, God?" I asked.

He said it again: "Turn around and give her that bag of snacks that you purchased."

I did what He told me to do. I drove next to her, and I said, "Hello! Can I offer you this?" I handed it to her, added, "Bless you," and left.

My heart felt good but after I drove off, I broke down like a little baby and wept for her. I kept saying, "Thank you, God," over and over. I just couldn't believe that He wanted to use me in all of my mess. I was humbled. I prayed that night and asked God to take the cigarette craving from me. "I don't want to wake up and put a cigarette in my mouth before my feet hit the floor," I told Him. I enjoyed smoking, I really did, but I knew it was not good for me and I didn't want to do it anymore. I wanted to live a saved, Christian life.

After crying out and asking God to take the cravings from me, I broke up all my cigarettes, flushed them down the toilet and went on to sleep. I woke up the next morning, and I didn't have a taste for cigarettes. I never picked up another one again. I couldn't believe it. In an instant, when all the times I tried on my own I could not do it, God did it. He is so amazing.

# Chapter 8

As good as God had been to me, I wanted to do everything I could to live right and be pleasing in His sight. It seemed like everything went my way when I first gave my life to Christ...everything but Dee! I couldn't understand why God would not let him out of my life all the times I asked. I just couldn't figure it out.

A month later, I found out I was pregnant during my annual checkup. I was in total shock! It had been around three months since I stopped sleeping with Dee. I still remember that night. I told him I wasn't sleeping with him without a condom. He was livid. He tried forcing me. I struggled, but he did not stop. I got tired of wrestling and let him have his way. And with the news of the pregnancy, I went into a depression once again. It wasn't that I didn't want my baby because children are gifts, no matter what. I just didn't want a baby *with him*. But I didn't want to get rid of it either. I chose to keep it and care for my child on my own.

When I found out, I was already four months along. I had been on birth control and still getting my menstrual cycle up until three months prior. When I went to the doctor, I told her that my period was a week late. I was on time like clockwork every month, so a week was a concern to me. When she came back in the room, she said, "Guess what? You're pregnant."

All I could do was tear up. I couldn't hold it back. She asked me if I was okay. I told her this was not planned, and I really wasn't planning on having any more children. My first born was eleven years old already. What I went through, and was still going through, with Tyrell was enough to handle. My son always said he wish he had a sibling, but I couldn't see how I would be able to care for another child. I told God then, "I need You. I can't do this without You." And God kept reassuring me that everything was going to be alright and to stop worrying. He had me.

My focus from there on was my pregnancy and staying stress-free. I told Dee I was pregnant. He said he was happy about it and acted nice for a little while. Then word on the street was that there was someone else pregnant by him as well. Things got back to me, and I am sure that he assumed it was Howie or Zelma. When I asked him about it, he had a shocked look on his face and said, "What? Where did you get that from?"

"Answer the question," I told Dee. "Where I got that from doesn't matter."

"No!" he said, and I left it alone, though I didn't believe him. After a while he stayed away and slept out more. I truly didn't care, because I was done with him and made up my mind to have my child and raise him without his father in our lives. I didn't want my son around him anyway. Dee had another son in New York. I remember one time he brought the baby to the house when we lived there. He was around one year old. The baby was crying, and Dee said, "Shut up man. You're not no girl, shut up."

I was so mad. I retorted, "Why are you talking like that to a baby?"

But he said, "Hush, no son of mine is gonna cry like a batty boy."

That was a term that Jamaicans used for a gay or effeminate man.

I remembered that and knew he would not know how to talk with my baby boy. This would always be an argument with us because I wasn't going to let Dee talk to my child that way. Dee staying away and out of our lives was okay with me. This was something I was willing to do without him. I talked to myself a lot and affirmed that things would be okay. My mind was so mentally drained, bruised with abuse, feeling insecure and beat down—and being pregnant didn't help. My emotions were all over the place. I found myself crying a lot and thinking of ways to get him out of my house once and for all!

I was around six or seven months along, asleep in my bed when I was awakened by the door closing and Howie running upstairs into my room.

"Nik," he said, "Come downstairs. Me and Cuz was robbed!"

I got downstairs only to see Clay standing over the sink, drops of blood all over the floor.

"What happened to you?" I asked.

He looked up and I saw he had a hole over his lip. I mean I could literally see through his lip. At that point, I panicked. I got some towels for him and to be honest, I don't even know what happened after that. I don't know if they went to the hospital or what. My stomach felt like it was contracting, and all I could do was pray, "Please, Lord, don't let me have another premature baby."

When we spoke later, I asked them what happened. They said they were in the store and some guys came in and robbed them. They hit Clay with something in the face, though the hole in his lip looked like a gunshot. They said that they didn't hear any guns. The first thing that came to my mind was that Dee had my family set up. I believed in my heart that it was him and even asked him about it the next day when I saw him.

"I know you had Howie and Clay set up to be robbed last night!" I told him.

"Oh, they were robbed? What makes you think I had something to do with that?" he said calmly. "I sure don't need nobody to do nothing for me, so don't come to me with that."

I walked away from Dee when I saw that he was happy that the situation happened. I couldn't stand him. How I felt about him was getting worse, so I needed him to go.

He was already halfway out, I needed him all the way gone. I was on the brink of a nervous breakdown. I cried many nights to God, but it felt like He was ignoring this one prayer and I could not figure out for the life of me why. I trusted God to protect me but was starting to get scared for my life and for Dee's—I was getting to the point where I actually thought I could kill him. I had a shotgun that he didn't know about. I purchased it and put it up in my closet behind my clothes. Eventually he found it, which meant he was snooping. He came to me with the shotgun and demanded to know, "What's this? What are you trying to do with this? I know you didn't get that to shoot me."

That pregnancy had me evil as well. I wasn't scared. I told Dee to get out of my face. "I'm really getting sick of you assuming things and coming to me with your mess. I live in a home and I can have a gun for protection, that's what I got it for. You're in the streets doing who knows what. I have to protect my family."

I knew better than to say that. He went off and started yelling and cussing.

"Why would I jeopardize you? Nobody knows where you live, and I made sure it stayed that way."

He stormed out angry as usual. My heart started racing and anxiety kicked in. I started to cramp. Every time I got excited, my stomach would tie up in knots. I was cramping off and on for about a week or so after that, so I stayed off my feet. I was home most of the time, just me and my little man. I was at a new job at the time (Cigna), and I loved being there. For one, Dee couldn't just come into the building when he wanted to pop up, which he didn't do anymore, thank you Jesus! Work was where I found my peace of mind. It was also where I met Christa. She was a coworker and an extremely sweet girl. We became fast friends and still stay in contact today. She is a forever friend and sister.

When I wasn't at work, I would take a ride to Virginia to see my mom. I loved spending time with her. I wanted her to come to North Carolina, but she decided to move to Virginia with her husband. That was okay since it gave us somewhere to go and get away on the weekends. The only thing I didn't like was that the time flew by so quickly. Before you knew it, it was time to get back in the car and drive back to Raleigh.

# Chapter 9

After visiting with my mom one time, I arrived home and prepared myself for another workday. I received a call from Clay that night. He and Howie had gone to New York to visit family. He let me know that he would be staying a little longer, but that my brother was on the way.

I got up the next morning and pressed my way to work. It was a beautiful, sunny day. I went out to get me a little lunch and ate outside since it was so nice. I was talking to God, still asking Him to let Dee come home and tell me he was leaving. But I was also telling myself affirming words, like things would be easy for me and that I wouldn't go through this alone. I would have great people around me and my children would grow up to be great and happy young men. I don't know where that came from, but that day started a habit for me of affirming things and I would feel better after I did. It wasn't an everyday thing, but whenever I started to feel a little down, that's what I would do. I would ask God to cover my family and keep us protected from any harm or danger that could come our way. My walk and my relationship with God were getting stronger and I was better for it.

I came in from work that day, took my shower, got comfortable and relaxed. I thought Howie might be there when I got home. I didn't see him, so I thought he either came in, showered, and went out, or he was still on the road. You know young men—they don't know how to bring their tails straight home. They must stop here and there.

That evening, I received a phone call from Clay. He told me that Howie was in jail in Virginia. My heart dropped in my stomach. I couldn't believe what he was saying.

"Come again?"

He told me the cops had stopped him and the two other friends that were with him. They took them in because they found drugs in his car.

I couldn't believe it. I cried all that night, wondering what was going to happen. When I finally spoke to Howie, I was so angry with him. I just couldn't believe that I was talking to my brother from jail. What was he thinking?

He made bail. I didn't have any money at the time to get him out of jail, so I had to put my house up as collateral. I didn't want to do it, but I did because I knew deep down in my heart that Howie wouldn't skip town, miss his court date, and jeopardize me losing my home.

It was Wednesday, June 13, 1999 when I bailed him out. I was carrying pretty big and was now eight months pregnant, wobbling all over the place. I was cramping and my back was hurting. I stayed home because it was hard for me to concentrate on anything but Howie being locked up. I hadn't told my mom yet about my brother because I knew that she would worry, and I really didn't want my mom doing that and going into a depression like me. I left that up to Howie to tell her. Especially since he had to go back to court.

Later that day, I was really cramping. It was probably around 5:00 pm now and the cramps were coming about every ten minutes. I was panicking now. I was praying and asking God, "Don't let me have this baby now! Let me go the whole nine months please." I was scheduled to have my son on August 24, two days before his father's birthday. You know I prayed that didn't happen.

I laid down in the downstairs bedroom and tried to take a nap to take my mind off the cramps, which I now knew were contractions. I was supposed to call my doctor if contractions were at least two to three minutes apart. I told myself these were Braxton Hicks contractions, not the real ones. I called my doctor anyway, just to let her know. But she was out of state. "Oh no," I lamented, "Please don't let me go into labor tonight! I want my OB-GYN doctor to deliver my baby."

I got up to make myself a cup of tea since the contractions weren't easing up. They were probably around seven to eight minutes apart now. I realized then that this was the real thing. I heated up the kettle and I felt warm water stream down my leg. My water had broken. My heart raced and I started to panic: Tyrell was spending the night at a friend's house and I was home alone with no one to assist me. I thought, 'Why am I always by myself when I go into labor?'

I called my girlfriend Sandie and she and her husband came and got me. I was glad that my water wasn't coming out as fast as it was when I had Tyrell. It was a light stream, but it kept on coming. My hospital bag was packed so I wouldn't be scrambling for it, but I couldn't even tell you where it was at the time. We found some plastic, lined her seats up and as soon as we got in the car, that fluid started coming out a lot. I told my girlfriend and she said, "You better not mess up my seats!" We laughed! But thank God we had that plastic, because I sure didn't want to pay to have her seats cleaned, even though I would have.

I knew I was having a boy already. I had found out at around six months because I was ready to start buying things for the baby. I wanted a little girl, but I guess God knew what I needed. That little girl would have been spoiled rotten.

We arrived at the hospital in around fifteen minutes. We went to Wake Medical since it was the closest to me; but by the time we arrived, I think all of my water was on the seat. I sure didn't feel much coming out when I stood up and sat in the wheelchair. They wheeled me straight up to my room and hooked me up to a heart monitor and made me comfortable. Zelma came by to the hospital. Sandie had to leave, but Zelma stayed to the end. Clay arrived from New York and came to the hospital as well. I was happy and a little down at the same time because I didn't have Howie to share in this joyous occasion.

Then Dee happened to call and check on me. I was surprised and didn't tell him anything beyond me being at the hospital in labor. He came by not too long after that. He saw Clay and my girlfriend there. His face became all screwed up and he told me, "You can tell them to leave now."

I did not do that though. Five minutes later, he said he was going to park the car because he left it in the front.

I said, "Okay."

He never returned.

I told Clay he could go on home and relax as he was just getting in from New York and he did. I was in labor for around six hours after my water broke. I told Zelma to call the nurse when I started getting the urge to push. They came in and told me not to push because I had to go to the operating room to deliver since I was only eight months pregnant. I guess they wanted to be safe than sorry, but I couldn't hold it. I yelled that to the nurse while they were wheeling me out and she yelled back for me to hold it, no pushing. She heard me moaning like I was pushing and said, "We're almost there. Hold on!"

We arrived and they got me ready for the birth. I had Damien at 3:00 am, Wednesday, July 14, 1999! He was so beautiful, with a head full of black hair. Damien only weighed four pounds and five ounces and had to stay in the hospital for two weeks. You know I didn't want to leave him, but two weeks were better than the five to six months that Tyrell had to remain in the hospital. I didn't complain. I was there every day.

Dee came too. It didn't matter to me if he did or not, but then I remembered I had heard another girl was having a baby by him as well. I chose not to put his name on my son's birth certificate. I wanted the Headecker name to live on, so that's what I did. When those two weeks were up, I was so happy to bring my baby home with me. His father was at the house during the day more that he usually was, trying to help. I was appreciative, but it was not needed. I knew how to handle things on my own. My mom came down to see her second grandchild. She was such a big help, such a good grandmother. She loved these boys with all that was in her, and they loved their grandma just as much!

The following month, my son's other grandparents came down to visit and see him. It was such a beautiful time. His grandma held and loved on him. She told him, "Meme (grandma in Jamaican) loves you so much." They were such a loving family. They loved me and I loved them.

# Chapter 10

I was enjoying my children and being a mom of two boys. They were my world, and I thanked God every day for them. They put a smile on my face and brought joy to my heart, even though I was broken inside.

My brother was now home too. I was happy to have him there; Howie was my world, and I wanted the best for him. I did not want him getting into the drug game, but he was no longer working at CarMax. He was just waiting for his court date.

Clay let me know that his girlfriend in New York was pregnant and he thought the right thing to do was to go back and be with her. I did not want him to go, but I understood and knew it was right for him to do so. He moved back and his girlfriend had a beautiful baby girl! I was so proud of him. He always kept his head in the right place and kept a job when he was in North Carolina. He went back to New York and did the same thing. As I write this, it's almost time for him to retire, and he's only in his forties! That's what I am talking about! I'm extremely proud of him.

When it was time for Howie to go to court, we didn't know what to expect. I was a nervous wreck. Then my brother was sentenced to three years in prison for drug possession. I was so hurt. All I could do was cry. I saw and heard all the stories about prison, and I did not want Howie going. I was messed up because now they were both gone: Clay went back home, and Howie went to prison. I started having anxiety and panic attacks again. I found myself slipping back into depression. My mother decided to come down for a week or two. The day she arrived, she settled down, sat at the table, and had a cup of tea. I went upstairs to use the bathroom and see why Dee had not come down yet to say hello. He was just sitting on the end of the bed.

"Go downstairs and say hello to my mom," I told him as I went to the bathroom.

Dee followed me in and said he didn't want to go. "You know I'm shy and don't like talking, and you know your mother likes to talk and ask questions. Don't get mad but I'm not going down. You know how I feel about being around people."

"She's not people, she's my mother and you better not be disrespectful and not go down and at least say hello to her, that's all I know," I told him.

Dee got mad when I said that and left the bathroom. I thought he was going downstairs, but he came back with a shotgun in his hand instead while I was sitting on the commode.

"You know you got a slick mouth. Why are you trying to make me do something I don't want to do? I'm not going down!"

"All you have to do is say hello, nobody asked you to stay and talk. That's my mom, not a friend. What are you doing with that (the shotgun)? You're talking too much, man, you don't know when to shut up." I said it again, "Go say hello to my mother."

Dee raised the shotgun up to my face. I don't know what came over me, but I exclaimed, "Do it! Do it please!" I was so angry. "Do it, so I don't have to see you no more!" I was scared but that's what came out of my mouth. He left, and I had to get myself together. I wanted to cry, but I was too livid to do so.

When I went downstairs. I asked my mom, "Did he say hello to you?"

"Yeah," she said. "He asked how I was doing, then left."

When evening came and it was time to call it a night, that was when I burst out into tears. I fell to my knees and cried like I hadn't cried before. Everything that happened earlier that day broke me down and all I could think about was what I said, telling Dee to shoot me. What if he had? I would have left my children behind without a mother to care for them, when I promised to take care of them and protect them. I begged and pleaded with God, "You have to do something. I am going to die, or he is. I need him to go! Please allow something to happen so that he can leave and get out of my life once and for all". I couldn't stop crying. But by the time I got up off the floor, I had a peace that was lingering over me. I didn't know what it meant, but I felt alright.

Dee came in later that night. This surprised me. I thought after he did what he did, he would stay out and away while my mother was there.

The next morning, I was downstairs with my mom, sitting at the table when he joined us and said hello to my mother. She talked to him for a little while I went upstairs to get Damien. I said nothing at all to him. He knew something wasn't right with me, but he was gone by the time I got back downstairs.

"Where did he go?" I asked.

"He just left," she replied.

"Good," I said. "He gets on my nerves not wanting to be around people."

"Don't stress that. You know if I have something to say I'm going to say it. I will go where he is, he doesn't have to come to me."

A couple of days later, I got up early in the morning to let my dog out to go to the bathroom. It was such a beautiful day out. My dog was running all around the grass enjoying herself, without a care in the world. I thought, 'What a great life that would be.' As I was gazing up to the sky and all its beauty, God whispered to me, "Tell him that your mother is coming to live with you and help you out for now."

"God, was that you?" I asked, unsure.

He said it again: "Tell him that your mother is coming to live with you and help you out for now."

I knew it was God after the second time. I didn't waste any time; I got right on the phone and told Dee what God told me to tell him (minus the 'God said' part).

"What? Help you out for what?" he demanded. "Forget it. Yeah, it's time for me to give you what you want. I need to get out of here and find me my own place."

I smiled as I hung up that phone. It was finally happening. Dee was already staying with one of his customers where he was doing his business, but now it would be official. I wasn't scared to tell him what God said. That was probably the peace that came over me when I got off the floor the other night. God was giving me peace and courage to not feel anxious, so that I could speak when I needed to. I didn't know if it would work, only God knew. I just obeyed and trusted God for the outcome. I remember thanking God and being so grateful that He was speaking to me and ordering my steps; and that I was listening. I told God, "If You do this for me, I will live for You and never go back." As difficult as this relationship was, it was because of Dee that I have a relationship with God. He is the one who brought me to my knees and to the Lord. This was the beginning of a true walk with God and trusting Him all the way with my life.

Dee came home later, sat on the chair in the room and said, "Can you pack my stuff for me? Just throw them in some garbage bags and I will put them in my car for now."

I said, "Sure," happy to do that for him.

He showered, got dressed and went right back out. He had two cars, one he drove and another one he had in the garage waiting for a part he had yet to get. I guess someone put it in their name because I knew he couldn't.

The time came for my mom and her husband to leave. I sure didn't want them to go, but they had their life there in Virginia. After all, God had me and my children. I spoke safety over our lives.

A week or so passed after I told Dee about my mother coming down. He was still in and out, but more out. I found myself getting frustrated because Dee hadn't found a place yet. He had his own room at his customer's house whom he paid rent in product (crack), so he had no worries about being homeless or anything like that. But he was still coming over. Three days later he called and said he was coming by to see his son. That's how he talked.

I told him no problem. But when he got to the house, he had a nervous look on his face, and he was pacing the floor. I saw him closing the blinds in the back and telling me to close the blinds in the front of the house.

"What are you doing? What's going on, and why are you telling me to close the blinds?"

"Just close them," he said, walking around with Damien in his arms.

"What is going on?" I demanded.

He waited a few minutes, then said: "Don't say anything, but somebody knocked on my door where I was staying and when I opened it, they tried to push their way in. They had a gun. I was able to close the door and get my gun. When I opened the door, they were running away. I just started busting as he was running. I think I hit him. I got my keys, got in the car and I left. I don't know if I killed him, he tried to rob me."

I was livid.

"Why would you come here?"

"I wanted to see you and my son."

I was a nervous wreck now. As careful as he had been all this time not letting people know where my home was, this was what he did?

"You gonna shoot and think you killed somebody and come here?" I exclaimed. I decided I had to leave. His mother had sent me some money through Western Union, and I was getting ready to go out to get it when he came by. I told him that, and he asked me to wait. I sat at the kitchen table with my hand in my head, exasperated.

Dee didn't like that. "Just chill out and let me think. I don't need you shaking your head and all that other stuff. I'm gonna leave, I just wanted to see my son." After a few minutes, he said, "Look out and make sure nobody is out there."

I did and saw no one. I took my baby and left. We went to Kroger's Supermarket down the road to the Western Union in there. On my way back home, a peace came over me again. I drove and sang. I was driving down Buffaloe Road, heading to Old Stage Road, the main street to my house, when a black van pulled in front of me, forcing me to stop. Another one halted behind me. I was scared out of my mind, wondering what in the world was going on.

*Part 4*

# God's Plan...
# My Whole Life's
# About to Change

# Chapter 11

I turned my music down and rolled my windows down to see six, big, old white men and one black man walking to my car. I saw their badges and guns and knew they were cops. One man asked me to step out of the car.

I obeyed.

"What is going on? What did I do?"

They pulled out a picture of Dee and asked if I knew him. I wondered to myself where they got the photo of him. That's one thing he didn't do: take many pictures of himself or let anybody else take one. I had never seen that picture before, but I confirmed who he was.

"Yes, I know him. He's my friend."

"Does he live with you?" they asked.

"No, he no longer lives with me." I told them that I kicked him out around a couple of weeks ago and he had been staying with that other girl.

"I need you to be honest with us," one police officer said, "Is he at your house right now?"

"Yeah," I responded. "He asked if he could come over to see his son and I said yes, but he was looking nervous when he got there. What's going on? What did he do?" I knew the answer already, but I wanted to know if the man he shot lost his life.

"He killed someone, and we need to apprehend him," he confirmed.

"He's there," I told them.

"Oh, my goodness," he said. "We have been watching your house for the last hour or two. There are cars in your subdivision, and we saw when you got in the car and left. His car was in the garage."

I was shocked to know they had been watching me.

They told me to describe the inside of my house: where each room was, and where the last place he was when I left. I was so confused yet happy to do so. While I did that, they looked in my car through the window and saw Damien in his car seat. They told me not to go home right now.

"No problem!" I told them. "Just go and get him out of my house."

They thanked me for cooperating with them. I wasn't going to lie. I was not getting in trouble for him. I was glad this was happening. I just couldn't believe what was going on. I was scared but so happy. The one police officer I was speaking to asked for my number and said he would call me when they were done so that I could go back to the house with the baby. I went to the local McDonald's and waited. It was probably thirty minutes or so before I got a phone call from the officer telling me to return home. When I got there, there were officers in the kitchen and upstairs, searching my house. They told me to have a seat.

"Did you all get him?" I asked.

"We think he must have spotted us out of the window. We saw the garage door going up when we got to the subdivision. He pulled out fast and a chase ensued," he explained.

"What? A chase? You mean to tell me you didn't get him."

"Ma'am, don't worry, he will not get away."

An officer came in through the garage. "Hello. Is that your baby?" he asked, pointing to Damien. "Cute little guy. I just left another lady's house. Her baby and yours look just alike."

I understood what he was trying to do. He was trying to get me mad so that I could talk and tell them whatever they needed to know. Little did he know, he didn't have to get me mad to talk. I was willing to tell them whatever I knew. The thing was, I didn't know much that I could tell them about Dee and his street life. He kept that far from me, where it belonged, in the streets.

The officer also said her house was where Dee lived with her. I was happy to hear that. When I told the other officer after they pulled me over that he no longer lived with me, I thought I was cleared of the living situation. But they insisted on looking through all my things. When I asked why, they told me, "We are looking to see if we can find the gun that was used in the shooting. He might have hidden it in your house."

I went upstairs, and found the officers in my room, going through my drawers. They said, "We're sorry, ma'am, we have to check. We've tried not to mess up anything up."

They eventually wrapped up after not finding anything. Then they asked me about the other car in the garage. Was it mine?

"No, that's his other car. It's open if you need to look in there."

"If you don't mind, ma'am."

They looked in the car. Dee had the clothes that I had packed up for him in there and all his belongings. When I told them he didn't live here, they believed that because they didn't see his clothes in my closet or drawers.

We went downtown after that. They kept me there for about an hour, questioning me. I told them Dee was abusive to me, and I wanted him to leave. I prayed for something to happen and God answered my prayers.

"I guess he did, ma'am," the officer said.

"You see Dee was no good. Look he went and had a baby with someone else while I was pregnant. You think I want to be with that? Oh, and for the record, tell your men to be careful because he can't stand cops and I'm sure it would be nothing for him to take one of you out. Have a nice night!" I added before leaving.

They had an officer waiting outside to take me back to the house. It was a long day! I went home, bathed Damien fed him and put him to sleep. I got myself together, ate a little something and laid on the bed. I cried and told God, "Thank you, Lord! I am forever indebted to You. I had no idea what was going to happen or how he would ever leave my life, but You did, and I thank You from the bottom of my heart."

I turned on the news and it was all over the television, who he was and what he did. They said he took the police on a high-speed chase (they shared my street address, though not my house number. I couldn't believe it. Why would they say that?) and crashed into someone's yard. When the police found his car, the people who owned the home said that he knocked on the door and asked if he could use their phone. I don't think they knew what was going on at that time. He was now on the run and considered armed and dangerous. He was on foot and they had helicopters on the lookout as well.

I was mostly upset that Dee got away, but I knew he wasn't coming back after all of this. I laid down, prayed, and went to sleep, exhausted mentally and physically.

All of this was on the news for a week. I bought the paper and cut out the article about him. I saved it, thinking when my son was a teenager, I would use it to explain to him what happened and why his father was not a part of his life.

I heard from the police twice after all of this occurred. Around three days later, I got a phone call. I wasn't going to answer it because it was a number I never saw before, but I did. It was Dee. He said, "I can't stay on this phone. I wanted to apologize for coming over there after this happened. I just wanted to see my son because I didn't know what was going to happen with me."

"How did you get away from the cops?" I asked him.

"I crashed into a yard and ran on foot, bare foot. Listen, I gotta go!"

I cannot remember if I gave the police the number that Dee called me from, but regardless, it wasn't a long enough call to trace. At that point, I never heard from the police again. Maybe they were in contact with his other baby's mother that he was staying with. Whatever it was, I was grateful. I did not want to be hounded by the police about this. I was actually more than just grateful. I was in awe of God. He was absolutely amazing. I thought about how God set this up and protected me. He told me tell Dee that my mom was moving down because God knew he would not stay. Then with me packing all his stuff up and getting it from the inside of my home, clearing it up— He knew what was about to occur...

I can't even explain the weight that had lifted off me. I felt like I could fly. I just wanted to go on with my life, enjoy my children, my home and most of all the Lord. I couldn't even enjoy my walk with the Lord when I was dealing with Dee. I felt like I was a double-minded person unstable in all my ways. But now I could focus and live the life I was meant to live. I told God, "Thank you, Lord, for all You have done for me so far. I can't thank You enough, only show You, and that is what I plan to do."

I never heard from Dee again, so I cannot say if he's still on the run or if he started a new life somewhere else. For myself, I went on to live a normal and stress-free life. I can't explain how good it felt to not hear the garage door going up at night, being awakened out of good sleep to argue and get accused of things that I didn't do; to smell stink liquor coming through what it seemed like was his pores and on his breath. I was so turned off with the smell of liquor and marijuana, I promised myself I would never deal with another man that indulged in drinking.

I dedicated my life to the Lord and my whole life was my children, work, and church. I went to church faithfully. I was growing closer to the Lord and learning more about Him. Since I didn't grow up in church, I was a late bloomer. But between Mama Butler and Mother McGhaney, I was able to turn to God. Mother McGhaney was a neighbor who lived downstairs on the first floor in my building in New York and wanted everybody to know Jesus and get their souls right with God. She held prayer services in her home, and would tell us to come on in. I never forgot that. I loved that lady.

Looking back, I realized that God had His hand on my life for a very long time, I just didn't realize it until I started thinking back on all the experiences I had growing up. Some of the things that I was speaking in my life when I was a young lady have come to pass as an adult. I always felt different growing up. I would see things before they happened, I would have crazy dreams that came to pass and tell things that I saw were going to happen. I didn't understand it, but I believe God's spirit rested on me as a teenager. My mother raised us to be respectful ladies and I never felt right doing something that was wrong. It never sat well in my spirit. Now I knew why.

# Chapter 12

I noticed that I started getting my appetite back and picking up weight, which I never really had when I was with Dee. I was small, probably a size 12 then. I looked older than I was because of the stress and stress will age you. Over the years, I went all the way up to a size 18/20, and that weight stayed on me for a long time. I was happy, no complaints here!

Damien was now two years old, and Tyrell was fourteen. It was time to go back to work. I left Cigna and started working for the state at the North Carolina Employment Security Commission. It was my neighbor, David, who told me to fill out an application and they would start me off as a temporary employee. I was a temp there for a whole year until applying for a position that came open in the Data Entry department. I applied, went for an interview, and got a call after a while that the position was mine if I wanted it. I told them, "Yes, I absolutely want it.!" My plan was to stay on that job for two or three years at the most. I had a wonderful supervisor named Joe. She was very patient with me and always mentioned the good Lord, which was alright with me. She let me know that her office was just a few steps away if I needed her. However, she developed breast cancer and left after a year of being my supervisor.

Remember I told you, in the beginning of your walk with Christ, it seems like this walk is easy and the things you prayed for, He will always give you. Well, I learned that wasn't so dealing with my son's father. I had to stay in that situation until God was ready to bring me out. This was all in God's timing, not ours. Well, after Joe left, a new supervisor was hired, Fee, and it was downhill from there. I don't know what it was, but she would speak but not smile. It seemed like she would look at me with a disgusted expression. I thought, 'What is going on here? I couldn't do that to anyone. It wouldn't sit well in my spirit to look at someone in disgust and barely speak for no reason at all.'

I went to work, did my job, and went home. As time went on, it seemed like I was being called into Fee's office every other day about something being done wrong with my assignments. I never had a complaint about my work until she became my supervisor. I don't know what it was, but she had it out for me. She was a sister, one of us, if you know what I mean, and sometimes your own kind will try and do you in. It's sad, but with everything that was going on, it seemed to me that God had me in a season of what I called 'looking like a fool.' I was going through so much even though I was the one living right and being good to everyone.

I recall on one occasion, a friend of mine needed to borrow money because her lights were going to be cut off that day. I didn't have the money, so I offered to take my $3,500 bracelet and pawn it for her. I simply asked her not to lose it. Long story short, it was taking her a long time to get my bracelet, so I called the pawn shop where she went, and explained the situation to them. They told me that my bracelet was in the showcase for sale. I was livid. I had to go to the shop to see for myself—my beautiful bracelet was on sale for $2,300. I only did this because she had a small child at the time, and I didn't want them in the dark.

I didn't call her after I found out. I told myself, 'I will wait until I see her at church and talk to her.' I did just that and said, "You lost my bracelet?"

She said, "No, what are you talking about?"

I told her my bracelet was in the showcase at the pawnshop for sale. She didn't believe me though and must have felt some way about me approaching her about MY bracelet because she got offended. When the next Sunday came, God told me to apologize for offending her. I could not believe it. She lost my bracelet, but I had to apologize to her because of how I approached her about my property. I felt so stupid that God had me do that, but I did it.

Back to the job situation: I went into work one morning and was stopped in the hallway by a lady who worked on another floor. She didn't know me well but said that she always saw a smile on my face when I walked by and that she wanted to tell me something.

"Keep this between me and you. Your supervisor talks with me a lot and she is the type that talks about people. I just wanted to tell you to be careful, because I don't know what it is, but I just don't like what she's doing. Fee is jealous of you. You come here every day looking like a million bucks, and some people can't stand to see that. She must have gone to the Wake County Property tax website and pulled up your address to see where you live. She showed me on the computer your home and started saying, 'She don't need this job, look where she lives, and she drives a big truck.' I asked her why she was looking up people's addresses and where they live. She said, 'I just wanted to know!' Be careful, she's out for you. She doesn't want you here. But you didn't hear none of this from me."

I thanked her. About a week later, I was called into the office of Fee's boss. She told me that she had been getting complaints from my supervisor that I was making a lot of mistakes.

"With all due respect," I told her, "I have never had a complaint about my work since I have been here. My supervisor does not like me, and I don't know why. She barely opens her mouth to speak to me, she looks at me nasty, and every other day she is calling me into the office saying I did this wrong, and I did that wrong. She is blaming me for my numbers being off, but I make sure I do my work accurately. This is people's money we are dealing with and I make sure I put the correct amount in all the time." I started tearing up at that point. "She has got to be going in and doing something to my work, please believe me. I have wanted to come to you about her attitude towards me for a while now, but I left it alone and dealt with it. Now that she came to you, blaming me for things I didn't do, it's only right for me to tell you how I have been treated by her."

I was going to leave the office, but God told me to tell her about what the lady told me. I thought, 'Oh my, she told me I didn't hear it from her,' but I did as God asked. I sat back down and told her boss what was told to me and what she was on the computer doing. I left the office and continued to come to work and do my job under a mean and jealous supervisor who didn't care for me. That was a hard thing to do, but I did it anyway.

I found myself having anxiety attacks and my spirit was getting grieved by what I was going through. I asked God, "Why am I going through this? I could see if I gave her reason to not like me, but I come to work smiling and always saying hello to her and everybody else. I have never bothered anybody on that job. I am always kind and loving to everybody."

God would not tell me why though. I had to go through it without an answer from Him. He just kept my mind sane in the midst of it.

Fee called me into her office a few days later. She was still complaining about me putting the wrong amount of money in.

"I was able to go in and correct or change things," she said.

"That can't be right," I insisted. "I take my time and make sure that I am putting the correct numbers in." I even told her that I had never been called into the office about my work being wrong until now. I didn't understand it.

"I don't understand it either, but the numbers don't lie,' she told me. "If this keeps happening, I'm going to have to make some changes that I don't want to make."

I left the office, upset because I couldn't say what I wanted to say and call her the liar that she was. I left it alone and went back to my desk and did my work. It was hard for me to concentrate because of all that was going on.

My two on-the-job girlfriends, Priscilla and Marchelle, were my backbone at that time. They kept me encouraged when I would vent to them about everything. Marchelle and Priscilla would tell me to ignore it all and pray.

"Everything will be okay," they told me.

Thank God for friends who can pray when it seems hard for you to.

I don't recall what day of the week it was, but I arrived to work and found out that Fee was no longer the supervisor of the Data Entry Unit. She had been demoted to data entry supervisor! I was surprised. I never wished ill against her or anything, even with all she was doing. I had asked God to move me, but He let me stay and He moved her instead. People need to leave God's children alone and keep their mouths off them. It was hard for me to come to work under those conditions, but what can you do when you can't leave because you need to work and provide for your family and keep a roof over everyone's head? You go and you put up with what you must, give it to God and let Him fight your battles.

I had only planned to stay at that job for two years, but it had now turned into seven. I was not happy at all at my place of employment, but I had to stick it out. God gave me that job and I was not going to leave until He said, "Go." He didn't open another position outside of the Employment Security Commission for me to go to though.

After about another year, I applied for and got a position within the company in the Document Processing Department. Things were good back there for a while. I got along with my supervisor. I'm not sure how long she was there, but she soon retired.

I believe every job has some people who will just not like you, try to be in your business and make you look like the bad guy. You just have to learn to take the bitter with the sweet. We were without a supervisor for a minute, then after a while someone was hired. She was a lady who worked in the building already on the same floor that I was on. She had been at the Employment Security Commission for a long time. Things were great in the beginning but then they started to change with her as well. She was nice to the other ladies but started to change with me. I just didn't understand it. I thought, 'Here we go again.' It made me mad to see how she was acting towards me.

She called me into the office one day and asked me if I was okay.

"You seemed to have changed and don't look very happy," she told me.

I wanted to tell her that I wasn't, because of her and her off-and-on attitude, but I always remembered what my aunt said: "When you walk around with a screwed-up face like you just ate a lemon, it makes the people around you mad." That is exactly what it did to me. Every time I looked at her and saw her face and her attitude, it made me have one. Energy is a very real thing, and you don't want that negative energy around you because it will jump on you and change your whole disposition.

Instead, I did my job and continued having problems off and on. You would think that if you have problems everywhere you go, you must be the problem, but that wasn't the case. It's sad to say, but this was a race thing and not the kind we talk about. While I was at that place, the white supervisor treated me better than the three black supervisors that I had. It hurts when it's coming from your own race. They treat you like you're inferior to them and abuse the authority that was given to them. I just can't understand for the life of me why some African American sisters who are given authority and power don't know how to use it in the right way: they abuse it and hurt those who work under them. It's safe to say that everyone is not supervisor material.

I am the type of person that no matter what, I always said good morning to my supervisor and everyone in the office. There was a coworker who was acting shady too right along with her. I came to work one day and said, "Good morning," as usual. She didn't say anything, so I went to my desk and started working. My supervisor came out of her office after a while. She went to my coworker's desk to hand her something, looked at me nasty and said, "Good morning to you too."

I told her, "I said good morning when I came in, you didn't say anything to me."

"If I heard you say, 'Good morning,' I would have said it back," she said, while she was standing in front of my coworker's desk. So unprofessional. A supervisor is supposed to take you into their office if they have something to say to you. Not this. I was livid after that. I prayed, and told God, "I can't take it anymore. I don't understand why I have to go through this. What do you want me to get out of this? What am I supposed to learn in all this? These people treat me bad, and they have terrible attitudes."

I was called into the supervisor's office after a while, and she said, "I told you that my door is always open. If you need to talk about anything you can do that. I asked you in here to talk and put things on the table. You come in here, you don't speak, and we feel like we have to walk on eggshells here with you."

"You're the one who's changed towards me, and when people do that, I stay to myself," I told her. "I don't know why people would have to walk on eggshells with me. I speak every time I come in, regardless of how people act towards me. So, if me staying to myself causes people to feel a certain way, there is nothing that I can do about that. One thing I will never be is disrespectful towards you."

"You and I have never had a problem. We'd see each other in the hallway and speak; or you'd stop in my room, and we would talk and chat. You have always been a sweet lady. I just can't understand the change in you."

"Well, I don't do the sometime thing. I am the same all the time, and always will be," I said.

We talked a little more and put everything on the table. Things were good from then on with us. The enemy came in and tried to mess up things, but I stayed the course again. Although I was ready to call it quits, I didn't. She retired a year later.

We were without a supervisor for a while again. They would post the position, but no supervisor was hired. Eventually one was, and she was cool. We had a disagreement one time, but she wasn't as bad as the rest. She was a sweetheart. She didn't stay too long, perhaps a year or two, then she moved out of state. We went without a supervisor for about a month, then they put someone from the same department to watch over the unit until they hired someone permanently.

# Chapter 13

It was now December of 2007 and my underarm had been bothering me for around two weeks. It felt like I put a little ball under my arm and left it there. It was very annoying to me. While I was in the shower, I was rubbing around under my arm to see if there was a lump, but there was nothing there. I didn't know what it was. Something told me to do a self-breast exam when I showered, which I never do. I was feeling around my breast and came across what I thought felt like a little lump in my left breast. I kept feeling and it was moving as I pressed. I wasn't too concerned because I just had a mammogram six months prior. I made an appointment with my primary care physician. just to be on the safe side though, to see if it was maybe a cyst or something.

My appointment day came. My doctor examined me and couldn't feel anything. I told him to let me find it. I couldn't feel it while laying down, so I sat up and felt it. I told him where to feel, but he said, "I don't feel anything there."

"It's there, feel."

He examined me and said, "Oh yeah, I feel a little something there, but I wouldn't be concerned with it, probably just a little cyst."

"Well, I want to get it checked further," I insisted.

He referred me to the Rex Breast Center to get an ultrasound done. They examined me and sent me to the waiting area. They called me back into the room after a while. The doctor came in and told me that my ultrasound looked suspicious. They wanted to refer me to a surgeon at Rex Hospital to get a biopsy.

Now I was panicking.

"What are you saying?" I asked.

"When ultrasounds come back suspicious, we like to check it further with a biopsy to make sure it is not cancerous."

All I could think was, oh my Lord, please don't let this be cancer!

They set my appointment up. I went to see the surgeon, and he did the biopsy. I don't know what kind of tool he used to do it, but if felt like a little drill and it hurt bad. It circulated and clipped some tissue from my breast. They told me they were going to send the sample out to a pathologist and as soon as everything came back, they would contact me.

It was now January 2008. I got a phone call from the surgeon at Rex Hospital. They scheduled an appointment for me the next day to go over my biopsy results. I went to the hospital the next day. I was by myself: my children were at school; Howie was locked up and I didn't ask any of my girlfriends to come with me. I sat down in the doctor's office and listened as he told me, "Your biopsy results came back malignant, which means you have cancer."

I put my head down and cried.

He put his hand on my shoulders and told me, "I know these are the three words that nobody ever wants to hear. We are going to take care of you, and you are going to beat this. You have one of those cancers that we call the garden cancer. What that means is that it's an easy cancer to treat. It's not an aggressive cancer, though we will treat it aggressively."

What kind of cancer is easy to treat when you have to treat it aggressively, I will never know, but I now had to be set up for surgery and then after that, to start treatment.

The time for my surgery came. I had my family there with me, had friends at the hospital who wanted to be there. I must give a shout out to Vilma Ratliff! She was my co-worker/friend who stayed with my family and by my side before I went into surgery and when I came out.

I remember coming out of surgery, not fully awake, but I could hear people talking (the doctor was speaking with my family). I also remember moaning, trying to get somebody's attention. While I was laying on my back on the gurney, I felt something funny in my breast area. For some reason, I was sure I saw my breast blowing up like a balloon and feeling tight. I moaned louder, and Vilma, my mother or the doctor heard me and ran over to the bed. I remember someone saying, "There's blood on the floor," and then the bed was moving. The doctor told my family that they had to get me back into surgery quickly. I didn't know what was going on, but they were rolling me fast. And then I was asleep again.

When I finally awoke after surgery, my family and friends came in two-by-two to say hello and let me know they were there. I was so grateful for them that day, supporting me and my family and wanting to be a part of the start of this cancer journey with me.

The doctor told me that they had to take me right back into surgery because I developed a hematoma. My left breast was filling up with blood and he said if they had not gotten me back into surgery when they did, I would have gone into cardiac arrest. He told me, "When we went back in, we found that there was still cancer in there and we didn't have clean margins (cancer wasn't removed all the way). Your breast was blowing up like a balloon, so we had to rush you right back into surgery after you came out of surgery." This was dangerous because I had to go back under anesthesia.

I was in the hospital for two days and then I was able to go home. I had bulbs coming out of my breast to drain any excess fluid that needed to drain out. My mom was there to take care of me, along with my beautiful aunt,

Theresa, and her friend Geraldine. I was in so much pain after the surgery that I could barely sit up on my own. I was at the mercy of my family. My aunt had to wash me up because I could barely move my arms. The doctor removed a sack of lymph nodes from under my arms as well. My friends and neighbors brought over food so that those helping me wouldn't have to worry about cooking. We were so thankful for the hearts of those who shared in this journey with us.

After a few days, I was able to move a little. The pain was still bad, but I forced myself to get up, move around and try to lift my arms as much as I could. A week passed and it was time to get my drains removed. That wasn't a good feeling, but I was sure glad to get it over.

My doctor was now Dr. Joellen Speca. She was a beautiful lady, who sat with me and told me what the protocol of treatment would be (Adriamycin, Taxotere and Cytoxan). She let me know that I would lose my hair, and that I would probably be nauseous and very tired after chemo, but that they would do everything they could to combat the symptoms.

Dr. Speca also said that my white blood count would be low and that I would have to come back the day after chemo to get a Neulasta shot. When your count is low, it's hard for the body to fight off colds and infections, so the Neulasta shot was supposed to help with that.

She gave me info for a support group at Rex Cancer Center in case I wanted to join and be around other women who were experiencing the same thing. I took the information just in case I wanted to give it a try.

I was out of work for a whole year so that I could go through my cancer treatments and begin healing. I wanted to get my body and life back to as normal as I could. It was now February 2008 and time to start treatment for Stage II ER/PR+ Her2- breast cancer. I had my appointment to have surgery to get my port put in. A port is a small implantable reservoir with a thin silicone tube that is inserted into the upper chest just below the clavicle or collar bone. A catheter is inserted into the jugular vein. The great thing about this, and the advantage to having it is that chemo medications and other medications can be delivered directly into the port rather than a vein, eliminating the need for needle sticks. I chose to get a port for that very reason, because it was difficult to find veins in my arms.

After the surgery, I noticed that my heart was fluttering a lot and I was coughing quite a bit. I told the doctor about it and how it wasn't a problem prior to surgery. I was told that they probably went down a little too far inserting the port catheter and that I had to have surgery again to correct that. I seemed to have no luck when it came to this.

A week later after the port surgery, it was time to start chemo. I went to the Cancer Center prepared to get my first treatment. My mother came with me. I was so nervous; my heart was racing when they called me back to the treatment room. I saw all the nurses with protective gear on so that the medications being administered to us, the poison, wouldn't get on them. Could you believe that they have to protect themselves from this horrible stuff that must go into our bodies? That was scary for me. One of the chemo medications that I was going to have to take, Adriamycin, was also called 'The Red Devil'. That's what makes you lose every bit of hair on your body, and I mean every bit of hair. I prayed before they administered the chemo, and I gave it to God. Just like I trusted God with other things, it was surely time to trust Him with this mountain I was about to climb.

I sat for four hours getting treatment. Everything went okay that day. We went home afterwards. I rested for a little while and felt okay. We woke up the next morning to go back to the Cancer Center to get my Neulasta shot to help my white blood counts not drop too low. We got back home, and relaxed. However, when the next morning came, I could not get out of the bed. I was so weak I could barely move. That was the start of my treatment journey. I was in the bed for at least a whole week, so fatigued, nauseous with barely an appetite. I could hardly get up to go the bathroom. I needed help. My legs were too weak to even push myself up.

We had to order a raised toilet seat to put on top of the toilet just so that I would be able to get up on my own and not have to bend my legs into a full sitting position. It was a tough first treatment; and by the time I felt better, it was time for the next one. I started losing my hair around the second or third treatment, so I had it shaved off. Seeing my hair start to come out was very emotional for me. I figured shaving it would be better than watching it fall out on its own.

I tried my best to live my life as normal as possible even through my treatments. My children were in school. Damien was in basketball camp. I would try to take him when I could; and when I couldn't, one of his teammate's mom would come and get him for me. My mom and aunt helped as much as they could. They would get on the road and come to North Carolina to take care of their daughter and niece.

The treatments were really giving me a hard time and I just wanted something to do to keep myself busy so that I didn't think so much about them. I decided to give the support group a try. When I arrived at my first meeting, there were around eight women sitting in the room. We all introduced ourselves and then they discussed what the group did, what they talked about and shared stories of their journey. I just didn't feel like I fit in there. All the ladies had to be at least sixty years of age and over. I was thirty-eight at the time and no one there looked like me nor were they my age. I never went back. The support group was a great thing, it just wasn't for me. I believe that because I had such a strong support system at home and around me, supporting me and speaking positively to me throughout my journey, that was all I needed.

I finished my chemo treatments, and it was now time for radiation treatment. I had to go to radiation every day for about a month or two. After the treatments, my breast and underarm felt and looked like I had second-degree burns. I did not know that radiation would do that to the skin. It was very grueling, but with the help of God and a great support system I made it through.

I was getting my last chemo treatment; and while I was sitting in the infusion room, God told me, "You will have your own company one day." I didn't doubt that, because I always wanted to have my own business and leave a legacy for my children; I just didn't know exactly what I would be doing. I knew I wanted to design clothes or luggage. I wondered too what the name of my company would be.

One day, I was sitting in the parking lot of the mall. I was getting ready to pull off, and God said, "Adove!"

I said, "Adove? What's that?"

"The name of your company!"

"What? What does that mean?"

"A DAY OUR VISION EMERGED!"

My mouth hit the floor. I couldn't believe it. I knew that was God because I would have never thought of that so fast. Later that year, he changed the pronunciation of Adove (a dove) to Adové!

I said, "That's it!" It sounded so much better. I was blown away and just wanted to see what God was going to do. One Sunday I went to church, and we had a guest preacher. They called me up and started telling me some things that God was saying. When this vessel of God told me that I wasn't the type to work for anyone, that I was a leader and they saw me working for myself, I was shocked. He was confirming some things that had been told to me by other people. As I was getting ready to walk away, the words, 'get ready to write your book,' were spoken. I just walked off and put my hands up.

# Chapter 14

I was finally done with chemo and finishing up my last radiation treatment. I went home, relaxed and put my feet up. Radiation drained me. I received a call from Sandie later that night. She invited me to a cookout that a family member was giving the coming weekend.

I said, "Sure, I will come."

I went to the cookout that weekend and enjoyed myself. It's always good to get out from time-to-time when you're going through a storm. I arrived home that night and received a call from Sandie soon after.

"I have someone who would love to meet you. Someone at the cookout asked, 'Who's that red bone over there?'" she said. I cracked up! "It's my cousin, Emmanuel. He wants to know if it would be okay if I gave him your number."

I really wasn't interested in anyone at the time. I was already committed to my walk with Christ and twelve years celibate. I didn't need anything or anyone to come in between that, but I told her, "Sure, you can give him my number."

Emmanuel called me, and we talked for hours on the phone that night, and the days to follow. He was a soft-spoken, country boy with a strong accent. To be honest, I was always turned off by a man with a country accent, but it didn't bother me like that with him. He was such a nice guy, and he loved the Lord. He was into church at the time. That was a check for me! I had asked God for a man of God who loved him, because I knew if he loved God, he would surely let God lead him and love me the right way.

We decided to meet up for the first time after conversing on the phone so much. I went to his family's house in Louisburg, North Carolina, and met his family. I was a little shy, but everyone was so loving that I felt okay after a while. I enjoyed everyone there. We didn't stay long. We rode back down to Raleigh and grabbed a bite to eat. We had a nice time. I was opening up to the idea of dating again. I was a piece of work when it came to men. I would not give them the time or day, and I'd talk so bad about them after my abusive relationship. But that was unfair to the others that might come along and treat me the way I should be treated. Never judge a man based on a prior relationship that didn't work out.

After a year of cancer treatment and going into remission. I decided to have a Celebration of Life cookout with family and friends. I invited Emmanuel to come along with Sandie. He came and we all had a great time that day. My mom and family were there. Some of my people from New York came to celebrate with me, and we just had a wonderful time. I was so happy to see everyone. When evening came, and it was time to end our celebration, some pitched in and helped fold tables and chairs and helped me put stuff up and away. It was a day to remember for me and a day I will never forget. Everyone left, and Emmanuel stayed and continued to help me clean up on the inside. While I washed dishes, he gathered all the garbage, rolled it up to the front of the driveway, swept and did whatever else his hands found to do. I hadn't experienced that in a long time. I forgot what it was like to have a man help out. I was grateful for him.

Emmanuel and I were inseparable after that night. We continued to date. I told him I had been celibate for twelve years and wanted to remain that way until I was married. He understood how important my walk with Christ was and respected those boundaries. We were together every single day, spending time, going to church, and getting to know one another.

When I met Emmanuel, I was finishing up the last part of my chemo and radiation treatment. I had on a beautiful lace wig that looked like my hair. I never took it off while we were talking. One day, God said, "Take it off and show him the real you."

"God, I'm bald-headed," I reminded him. "That might be a turn off to him."

"Take it off."

I went into the living room where Emmanuel was, and I told him that I wanted to show him something. I said, "You know I'm fighting cancer, right? Well, I just want to show you that..." I slid my lace wig back "...I don't have any hair."

He looked at me and said, "I don't care about that!"

I was blown away! I thought me having cancer would scare him off and we would just remain friends. I went upstairs to sleep later that night (Emmanuel was in the guest room). I laid in the bed talking to God.

"Is this my husband?" I asked him.

But he didn't answer.

"If it is, give me a sign. Tomorrow, let him mention something about marriage."

I woke up the next morning and cooked breakfast, Emmanuel was in the living room watching television. I don't know what he was watching but it must have been about getting married, because he came to the kitchen and asked me, "If I asked you to marry me, would you?"

My mouth opened wide. I wasn't expecting that. But I quickly told myself, "Maybe you thought that was a sign, Nikki! What do you know...?"

God knew though. We were married a year later on July 12, 2009. If Emmanuel stayed with me while I was battling cancer, and bald, I knew he was the one God sent. We had a beautiful wedding with lovely people sharing in our joyous occasion.

That brought me back to the time when my friend Doris called me. She said that she needed to come over and tell me what God had said and showed her. This was a year before I met my husband. She came by, we sat on the couch, and she said, "Girl, God said you are getting married! He showed me you in your gown and everything. It's going to be to a dark-skinned man, not skinny, but a medium-built man."

I told Doris, "I am not marriage material, darling! I love my privacy. I love going as I good and well please, and most of all, I love not having to answer and check-in with someone to let them know where I am. Besides, I don't think a man would be able to deal with me now."

Six months passed after Doris told me what God said. I remember I was in my closet cleaning and straightening it up and God told me to clear half of the closet out and put nothing there.

"Come again God?"

"You heard what I said. Clear half of that side of your closet out."

I could not understand for the life of me why he wanted me to do that, I felt like I was tripping. But I just shook my head, did as I was told and continued to clean. Then one day I was cooking dinner. God said, "Set the table for four."

"What did you just say, God? It's just me and my two boys, why am I setting the table for four?"

He didn't answer me the second time. I knew to just do it, so I did.

There was one other time I was cooking, and God said it again, "Set the table for four." I heard his voice and did what he told me. I remember him then saying, "I am preparing you for a husband."

I was shocked.

"WHAT?"

Then I remembered what Doris said. I just couldn't believe it. I had to do that for six months!

Now married, I understood why God had to prepare me. I always said I wasn't going to get married, I wouldn't date a country man, etc. Never say what you won't do because God's plan is not ours. God knew everything that was before me and knew I would need someone in my life to go through these things with. My husband has been with me through the ups and downs, some good and some bad. I lost my mom on Mother's Day 2012. Who would have thought I would be without my mom? God knew; and I am grateful that He loved me enough to set my husband right by my side.

After I lost my mother, my whole world was turned upside down. I couldn't fight the depression I was feeling, and I would cry from the gut many days missing her so much. Thank God for my husband who was there to comfort me. I suffered for quite a while. I sold my home because I didn't want to see the room that was hers when she visited, and just didn't want to be there anymore knowing that she would not be coming here to stay with me and her grandchildren anymore. I felt like I was spiraling downhill. How was I going to make it through life without her?

I would cry out to God to help me. As much as I trusted Him, I was still stuck in a state of what I felt was no return. I went to church one night. Apostle Debra Brown was the guest preacher. I can't tell you how instrumental she was in my life, even before my mother's passing. She called me up front and prayed that spirit of depression off of me. I screamed and cried out, and my spirit was free from that night on. I am grateful to God that He used her to change my life and allowed me some normalcy again. My husband allowed me to grieve in the way I knew how, but when the grief became unnatural, our Apostle stepped in. There is natural grief and unnatural grief. When you can't get rid of the grief and it overtakes your being, that's unnatural, and that's where I was!

I have been with Emmanuel now for eleven years and we have forever to go! I cannot tell you how happy I am that I listened to God when He said He was preparing me for marriage. Some may think it's strange that God would do that. Well, let me tell you, yes, He will! He will take the foolish things to confound the wise. You just have to be willing to look crazy in order to get the things that God promised you. I can't say that He will tell you to do the same thing that He told me to do. I will say though, just be obedient.

My husband is the best thing that ever happened to me besides my children. Be open to loving again regardless of what you have been through in your past relationships. All men are not the same. You don't want to miss out on what God has for you. All the things I wasn't looking for in a man were the very things God sent my way. God doesn't always send what you want, but He will send you what you need. I was grateful that God gave me a little of both. He absolutely sent me what I needed, and He surely sent me some of my wants. Be specific with your prayers and tell the Lord what you want in a husband/wife. Emmanuel can deal with my funny ways, and I can deal with his! We even each other out. We are balanced, and we love one another and have vowed to stay together for better or worse, in sickness and in health. My husband has kept his vows, and I sure will keep mine.

# Chapter 15

After I finished my treatment, I went back to work, and watched as the trouble started up again. It was the same as before. Things were so bad that I felt like I was on the verge of a nervous breakdown. I had to bite my tongue and not give the ladies a real piece of my mind. I found out over the years of dealing with anxiety and panic attacks, that holding things in was my biggest enemy. It caused me to get sick.

I was so hurt one day when I came into work and found out that one of my bridesmaids was talking about my husband. I let her stay with us for a week because she worked far from the job. I was being nice and helping her save some time and gas while she was going through a difficult time. Well, she cooked one night. I was on my way to bible study, and Emmanuel was upstairs. When he didn't eat any of her food, she felt some kind of way and decided she needed to tell people at the job about that, how he was too good to eat her cooking. My husband is very picky and does not eat everybody's cooking, friend or not. Well, it got back to me, and I didn't even say anything. I was just short with words and decided I didn't need friends like that in my life.

What do you know, one morning on my way to work, God said, "Go and apologize to her."

Of course, I argued with God.

"No! I didn't do anything. I am not doing it; she needs to apologize to me. Why do I have to look like a fool again and I didn't even do anything."

Can I tell you? As soon as I said that I saw there was a car on the other side of the divider going in the opposite direction, out of control. I knew that car was going to crash. Even though it was not near me, I decided to get in the other lane, but I couldn't because cars were too close to me and wouldn't let me over. I looked up and saw the out-of-control car was heading straight to me on the driver's side. I screamed, "JESUS!"

Somehow, the car jumped the divider and was side-by-side with me facing the same way I was driving. I can't tell you how that happened! This is something that you see on television or in the movies. My whole life flashed before me and I thought I was going to die that day. I said, "Okay, God, I will apologize." When God says to do a thing, don't question Him, just do it! This was the first time I told God I was not going to do what He said. I was tired of looking foolish and having to be the bigger person and say sorry to people who did me wrong. But when God tells you to do something, just do it. People who don't have a relationship with God and don't know Him and what He does, might think that this is foolish, and that God wouldn't do anything like that. But let me tell you, God will do what He has to do to get the attention of His children, especially those that He is preparing, shaping, and molding. God has to break you out of your ways so that you can be more like Him. When He allowed that car to spin out of control and head right at me, He got my attention. I remembered that my obedience to God was better than me sacrificing and not doing what He told me to do.

For example, I went to work another day and did what I always do: I got my work prepared, settled in, and then got ready to go down to the cafeteria to get breakfast. I started arguing with one or two of the co-workers because, as I was leaving the room, I heard them talking about me. I tried, but I just could not hold it back anymore. A friend who worked down the hall said she heard the commotion from where she was sitting. When she saw that it was me, she was shocked. She had never seen that side of me.

I started applying again for jobs internally, which I said that I was not going to do, but I needed to get out of there. I went to management, asked them to place me somewhere else because of what was going on, but they said they couldn't do that. They just didn't want to. They would make exceptions for who they wanted to make exceptions for and that is why I knew my time was limited there. I had to stay there and suffer! God did not open another door and allow me to leave.

Months went by, and I was still miserable while dealing with the immaturity of other people. I gave up trying to change the situation and asked God to give me peace until He moved me or them. I had to affirm and speak some things into the atmosphere. I kept telling myself that it would not be long. God was working on my behalf; doors were about to open.

My apostle at the time would tell me that she didn't see me there long, and another apostle told me the same thing. I believed them, because I knew there had to be more for me than staying couped up in an office building and not being able to connect with others. I didn't feel right there anymore. I trusted God and knew that there was something bigger. I told God, "Whatever it is, you get the glory because I don't know what to do in this situation."

A month passed after the incident. I was sitting at my desk, and I don't know what came over me, but I went downstairs to the mailroom, got two empty boxes, came back to my desk, and started cleaning my drawers out. I had very little left on my desk. I know everyone was wondering what I was doing. I was wondering the same thing. I don't know where that came from. All I know is that I felt like my time was really coming to an end there.

A month later, I received a call about a job that I applied for on the same floor, different department! The supervisor told me that the job was mine if I was still interested in the position. Can I tell you I smiled from ear to ear! I had packed up my stuff, not knowing what I was doing it for, and a month later I got a call for the new position. I thought I was heading out the doors of the Employment Security Commission, but I guess God had other plans, as He usually does.

# Chapter 16

It was now 2015. I had started my new position and had a wonderful supervisor. Jane was so quiet and a joy to be around. She had such a sweet spirit, that of a nurturer. She was extremely helpful and hands-on when it came to training me. She was there for a year and then applied for another position.

We were without a supervisor for around a month, and then a lady who was in the same department and worked with me, applied for the position and was now our new supervisor. Things were rough in the beginning and middle of the first year after she was promoted. The good thing about that is, I wasn't the only one who experienced her other side: we all had a problem with her attitude. She would come into the office sometimes and barely speak to us. After a few complaints about her from myself and coworkers, we had several meetings with our supervisor and her superior. We placed everything on the table and let our feelings out. As a result, we developed a better relationship. We had a couple of private conversations in her office, and she opened up to me about the things she was going through at the time. I would tell her about some of the things I was going through and we would pray for one another and lift each other up. Peace resided in the office and we were okay. I considered her my sister in Christ. We never know what people are dealing with in their private lives. That's why it's always good to remain humble and to be more understanding, not so quick to judge.

Another year crept on by, and an opportunity presented itself to me and my husband—a part-time job cleaning daycares after work. Emmanuel and I gave it some thought and decided to give it a try. We could use the extra money and we would be working for some great friends. It lasted a whole year. I was tired but I stuck it out and continued to push.

It was now 2017 and we were still hanging on in there at the second job. I was so proud of myself. But it started wearing on me. I would get up in the morning, go to my 9-5 and my body would hurt. It started in my lower back and eventually went to my upper back and shoulders. My hands and feet started bothering me. I thought, 'Okay this second job might be breaking this body down.' I continued to work though, still hurting daily and pushing through the pain.

I had to make an appointment after a while to go to the doctor. They didn't see anything wrong, sent me home and told me to take some Ibuprofen. And that was just about all of 2017, going back-and-forth to emergency rooms in excruciating pain with no relief. I got tired of all this. Eventually, my primary care doctor referred me to a rheumatologist to get checked. It had now been eight months of suffering, and he diagnosed me with Fibromyalgia! I thought, 'Great, at least I now know where the pain is coming from.' But it was getting worse.

I remember being very aggravated with my primary care physician after that. I had been with him for over five years but the best he could give me was, "You have Fibromyalgia; you have to take pain medication for that. There is really nothing I can do about it."

I was upset and felt like no one was listening to me. I found another primary care physician, but I didn't like her energy during our first appointment. She didn't smile, didn't extend her hand, or introduce herself. She was just too cold for me. I knew I wasn't going to be with her long, but since I was there, I explained my situation. She checked me out then sent me to get bloodwork done. I left there and prepared myself to go to my second job.

I got to the daycare, but I couldn't even lift my arms to clean the windows on the door or clean the little kids' toilets. I couldn't clean or vacuum the rooms. Everything became too difficult. I had to take a couple of days off to rest.

My new doctor had me redo the bloodwork. When the results came back, she said that I was showing signs of liver and bone disease. My liver enzymes and my Alkaline Phosphatase were extremely high. She told me she wanted to set me up for a bone scan and liver ultrasound.

I wasn't sure how to feel. I knew I had degenerative bone disease in my back from a while ago (I was diagnosed in 2005), but I wasn't sure about the liver disease. I wasn't a drinker, so where did that come from? I was scared but I tried my best not to panic and just get the tests done. I did both of those on a Thursday and scheduled an appointment with my doctor on Monday. Before I left the office where I got my scans done, the receptionist told me that I could download the patient portal and that would allow me to get all the information about tests and visits. When I got home, I downloaded it so that I would be able to see all results from tests I might take later.

I went to work the next day, but the pain was worse. I tried to get up from my chair, but I couldn't. I had to ask my coworker to help me up. He had to lift me off the chair. I could barely walk to the bathroom, that's how bad things had become. I left my job early and I went home and got in the bed. I woke up later that night. I don't know what made me check the patient portal, but I did, and I saw the results were already posted up there. I read them and then said, "Let me read that again."

*...too numerous to count, widespread osseous metastatic disease...*

I really didn't know what that meant, but I also knew I didn't like the word disease. Then it hit me! I remember seeing the word 'metastasis' before, and it had something to do with cancer. I looked up the words that I needed to know the definition of, and by the time I was done, I had a lump in my throat and my heart was in my stomach. It was widespread cancer. I panicked and was a mess for the whole weekend. I kept saying, 'Please don't tell me I have widespread cancer. I know that is not what these results are saying.' I was on edge all weekend and could not think of anything else. I also couldn't understand how they could put that on the patient portal before they spoke to the patient. Didn't they know the patient might pull up the results of the test without understanding fully what they meant?

# Chapter 17

Emmanuel made plans to come with me Monday morning to the doctor. We sat down and she still was not friendly, nor did she smile. I was just too through with her. She pulled her stool up to her desk, but I didn't give her a chance to say anything, I spoke first: "I happened to go to the patient portal and saw the results of my bone scan and liver ultrasound. I worried all weekend because I saw the words 'widespread metastasis'."

She said, "First let me apologize because I told them to not post the results. I told them I would go over them with you when I saw you on Monday. That was a mistake and was not supposed to happen."

"Okay, so are these results saying that I have cancer and that it's widespread," I said.

"Yes, you have cancer," she said.

"What exactly is it saying?"

"You have widespread metastatic disease that has spread throughout your bones and into your liver."

She stared at me after that and said nothing for a while. I was heartbroken, and scared. All I could do was cry. My husband and I just hugged each other and cried. After I got myself together, I was ready to leave her office.

"You will have to see an oncologist and they will handle things from here. There is nothing else that I can do."

I left her office, feeling like my life was forever changed. We were in shock. We couldn't believe it.

I made an appointment with my oncologist. We did a biopsy on my liver and then one on the coccyx bone. I felt the biopsy on the tail bone, but it wasn't so bad on the liver. I was sore for days afterward. After the biopsy came back, my oncologist let me know that I had Terminal Stage IV Metastatic Breast Cancer. The cancer had spread from the original site to other organs in the body. It usually metastasizes to the bones, liver, lungs, and brain.

"There is no cure for this type of cancer, but we can treat it to slow down progression," she told me.

I cried some more. All I could think about was that I didn't want to die and leave my children behind.

"I'm not ready to leave this world and leave my husband," I told God. "I love living, and I love life."

Dying consumed my every thought, every minute, and every hour of the day. I really felt like the depression was going to kill me before the cancer did. I felt helpless. I could barely do anything for myself because the pain had me feeling crippled. My husband, my sons, and my brother would help me get dressed, make it to the bathroom, etc. My son brought me a cane to help me get around. I barely used it. I didn't want to have to depend on it. I also had to wear a cap most times because I couldn't even lift my arms to do my hair or put on a little makeup. My sister and her husband came down and helped too. I loved them so much and appreciated that they always talked positive and let me know that everything was going to be alright.

"We will keep praying," they told me.

I was tired of feeling defeated. I cried out to God to please let me see my forty-ninth birthday which was in two weeks. When I was diagnosed with Terminal Stage IV Metastatic Breast Cancer, I was told that the median survival rate was twelve to thirty-six months. I was also told that people can survive three to five years, but everyone is different. The truth was, I didn't want to know how long I had. I talked to myself and said, "Nikki, by the time your forty-ninth birthday gets here, you will be a new person with a new mindset. You are either going to succumb to this diagnosis, or you are going to live with it and fight". I chose to live!

When my birthday came, I cannot tell you the peace I felt, but God did it again: He allowed me to see another year, and I promised Him I would not go back to that woe-is-me mindset ever again. I got out of that bed, I started smiling, and affirming what my life would be, and I started a 'Live List' of all the things I wanted to do before

God called me home. I was a changed person after my forty-ninth birthday. I continued to speak over my life, and I began to say affirmations and encourage myself daily.

We were now under the leadership of Bishop Ronald Godbee and Pastor Karla Godbee of the River Church in Durham, North Carolina! Can I tell you how much I love these two gifts from God and my River family? I don't know what I would have done without them. There are not enough words that I can say to let them know how much I love them and how grateful I am for all that they have done! Covering and praying for me and making sure I wanted for nothing. I am forever thankful. They helped me realize that my life was worth fighting for, and I promised myself I would do it until the end. My children deserved to see me fight and win. I would never give up or in.

I started adding to my 'Live List' and check off each thing that I wanted to do within five years. I wasn't trying to conquer my goals before I passed away. The truth was, I wasn't planning on going anywhere. I gave myself five years to fulfill my list because I didn't have a long list of things that I wanted to do. I figured I could do one thing a year. I wasn't going to go by the statistics of medical doctors for my life. God holds my life in His hands, and when He's ready for me to go, that is when I plan on leaving this earth.

I was ready to live my best life and not do what I did best—procrastinate. Situations like these are wakeup calls for us to stop putting off tomorrow the things that we can do today. A diagnosis of Terminal Stage 4 Cancer will make you enjoy the time that you have and live the most exciting life that you can.

I gave up my part time job and was now on medical leave from my full-time job. I continued to go to church as much as I could. My Bishop and church family continued to pray and lay hands on me. I was looking really bad at one point. I went from 250 pounds to 167 pounds in a three-to-four-month period. As much as I wanted and needed to lose weight, I sure didn't want to lose it because I was sick, but I had no appetite and was very immobile. I couldn't do much at all about that. My C4 vertebrae in my spine had collapsed due to the cancer and caused me a great deal of pain. I had to walk around with a neck pillow that had a draw string and tightened up just to keep my head stable. It hurt so much to move my head. I just couldn't do it. I also had to wear hats for around two months and no makeup because it was too hard to move my arms and do my hair and face. I was so miserable then.

One day when we went to church, Bishop told people to come up who needed a healing. There were around ten of us who went up there. He was on the stage and remained there going down the line. When he got to me, he didn't pray for me. Emmanuel was up there with me because at that time I was having a hard time walking on my own. Bishop told me that he would not pray for me.

I looked at Bishop, confused. I wanted to say, 'What?! I know you didn't just say you're not praying for me. What's your problem?" How was he going to get to me and say he wasn't going to pray for me? What did I do? I still loved my Bishop, but if I could have moved, I probably would have jumped on that stage, grabbed Bishop's hands, and laid them on me myself. I wouldn't have done that in reality but that's how I felt!

Then he told my husband that my life was in his mouth, and that he was to pray over me every day before he left the house to go to work.

After that, my husband prayed faithfully for me. I cannot tell you how much better I was feeling. I was so grateful for Bishop Godbee and Emmanuel's obedience.

# Chapter 18

I went to my appointment with my oncologist to discuss my treatment plan. I was going to start with chemo pills first. I was not excited about the treatment. You read so much on the internet about treatments, symptoms, and the side effects they cause that you don't want to go through any of it. If you are the type who will get spooked out by reading things, stay off the internet. Trust God and believe that your doctor is making the right choice for you. This is for those who are not doing alternative and holistic treatments. You still must do your research with everything, but sometimes we just need to stay off the internet, pray and do what is best for us. I also thought about how I felt when I was on chemo in 2008 and how I was bed-ridden for a week and a half, not able to move from extreme exhaustion, nausea, and body aches. All those thoughts came back to me and I just wasn't ready to experience it again, even though I had been cancer-free for ten years. You never forget your experiences.

But I wanted to live, so I had to go through with my treatment in order to get the best outcome for a better chance at living. I prayed, and I asked God to remove the fear so that I could fully trust this process of my journey. I believed God, started my treatment regimen, and did what I was supposed to do. I trusted my doctor as well. She was with me in 2008, and she was with me now.

I was also on pain management. I was prescribed Oxycontin and Oxycodone that I had to take daily. I stayed on pain management for about a month before I noticed a difference and did not suffer in daily pain. I eventually took myself off the Oxycontin because I did not want to become addicted to any of the pain meds. I found that when I stopped the Oxycontin, I was experiencing what felt like creepy crawlers moving up my arms and legs. I think these were withdrawal symptoms. It took about three days for me to not feel like that anymore. I'm glad I stopped when I did. I also eased up on the Oxycodone when I wasn't in daily pain. I started taking it as needed and I let my doctor know on my next appointment.

As I started to feel better, I looked on my Live List to see what I wanted to do first. On the top of the list was 'Visit Miami', which I always wanted to do. Also:

- Visit the Pink Teacup in New York.
- Take my kids to visit St. Thomas and meet their relatives.
- Co-host a show on television.
- Record a single.
- Meet Tyler Perry and land a role on one of his television shows or movies.
- Go to Los Angeles and shop on Rodeo Drive.
- Go to Los Angeles to spend a weekend or week with Tracey Edmonds.

Tracey will forever have a special place in my heart. We met on social media and talk and text from time to time. She always lets me know how proud she is of me and that she is always praying for me. She is my sister/friend, and her spirit is amazing. She is stuck with me!

That is my Live List, short and simple. I emailed some talk shows, and one of my favorites at the time was GMA Strahan and Sara which was fairly new on television. I couldn't believe that they replied to my email. I was excited before I even knew what they were emailing me to say. It could have been a 'thanks-for-your-email-but-we-will-not-be-able-to-fulfill-that-request' message for all I knew. I opened it and they said they loved my story and would love to be the one to make that dream come true.

In February 2019, I was on GMA Strahan and Sara as a third co-host. I can't explain the feeling and how much of a great time I had on that show. Michael and Sara were so down to earth, I felt right at home. People said I was a natural.

Since I wasn't feeling too bad with the treatment, I decided to make plans and conquer Miami second. My treatment did cause fatigue, body aches and nausea, but I made it through. My sister made reservations for us at a hotel in Miami and booked our flights; and in July, we flew to Ft. Lauderdale. We got to the airport, rented a car, and went on our merry way. The hubbies stayed back to animal-sit and work. Tyrell came with us and we enjoyed ourselves. I found out that they just opened a Pink Teacup Miami, so I was able to check off three things in one year from my Live List.

At the Pink Teacup Miami, we met the owner, Lawrence Page, and had a nice, peaceful lunch. We arrived early before the crowd came and were able to enjoy our time. The fried chicken was so good, along with the waffles. I don't know what he seasoned that chicken with, but I gave them two thumbs up!

I was not looking forward to getting back on that plane to fly home. I was terrified of flying and we had some turbulence on the way. When it was finally time to leave Florida, we took the car back to the airport, boarded our flight and headed back to North Carolina while my sister headed back to New York. Can I tell you that I thought we were going to meet Jesus on the flight? There was so much turbulence that Tyrell, who is a world traveler and not afraid to fly, thought he was going up yonder to be with his Lord. He was holding my hand, and I was squeezing his. Panic attacks started. I had pins and needles all through my body, my heart was racing. I was a nervous wreck until we landed. I got off that plane, thanked God and said, "I don't think I will be flying anymore; I'm just going to have to drive places, and wherever I have to fly to get to, I just won't see that place, and I am so fine with it. One day I might conquer that fear, but right now, I'm good. LOL! I will just focus on building my brand and finishing up my Live List within a five-year period."

We arrived home, talked about that flight, and Tyrell even said he didn't think he would be flying for a long time. Even the stewardess was scared. She tried her best to play it off, but it didn't work. She had the nerve to kneel down right near us. She tried to comfort us by saying,

"This is normal. We are going through a storm." That didn't help me at all! Bless her heart though, she tried.

I had to prepare myself for treatment the next day, so I showered, got comfortable and checked on my sister. She had some bad luck too. She had to stay at a hotel during her connecting flight due to bad weather. She was so aggravated. She didn't make it home until the following day. I felt so bad for her. I know all she wanted to do was get home to her husband and animals. She said she didn't think she would be flying for a while either. We all were through with it.

I woke up the next morning, arrived at the cancer center, did my bloodwork, and got my Xgeva shot to help strengthen my bones. It was also time to schedule my scans to see if the medication was working. The office called me to let me know that my markers were elevated and after my scans, my oncologist would decide what to do. I went for my scans and it showed progression on my liver. My doctor suggested a new treatment because of this. This was now going to be my 4th line of treatment. I wasn't happy. I felt down because I knew if this medicine that I was currently on didn't work, I was going to have to go on IV chemo next. I had to get over it quick and do the next line of treatment.

It was now September and I was preparing myself for the unknown. People with metastatic disease live in a constant state of the unknown. We never know what we are going to hear and what the doctor is going to tell us they saw. We hope to hear that there is shrinkage but a lot of times, we may hear progression. If you have never been sick, you will never know what it feels like to live with an illness that is like a rollercoaster, with up and downs. Be empathetic with people who are going through sickness. We don't want to be a burden to others, but sometimes the cards that are dealt are not the hand we choose. Be patient, show love and compassion. Not everybody is exaggerating about their afflictions. Some people are truly having a hard time with what they are experiencing.

# Chapter 19

We sat down with Dr. Speca and discussed my next treatment plan and what to expect. Tyrell was amazing! He was behind the scenes researching and reading up on my cancer and all the treatments that were being offered. He asked my doctor so many questions that she asked him if he was a researcher. I was shocked just like her. I guess he wanted to know what was down the road for his mom. My son didn't like to see me hurting and in pain. He just wanted to see me well all the time.

When I went through my cancer treatment in 2008 with my first diagnosis, I didn't initially show Damien my bald head. One day, I decided it was time for him to see his mom without hair. I sat him on the couch, and said, "I want to show you something babe. You know I'm going through treatments for cancer. Cancer can cause certain things to happen to your body. Treatment made me lose my hair." I took off my lace system to show him my head and he screamed and ran upstairs and cried. He was eight years old at the time. I knew he would be the one who wouldn't handle things well if I was sick.

While Tyrell didn't want to see me sick, I think he did come to handle things better and was willing to do all he had to do so that his mom would have the best quality and quantity of life. He told me he didn't know what he would do if he lost me. I worry about that as well. My children are my world, and I would never want to leave them under any circumstances. I'm sure we all wish that we could live forever but that's not possible. We need to enjoy life while we are here.

My motto after my diagnosis was to #LiveLifeLimitless and that is what I planned on doing. I wanted to live and make memories with my family and friends. Life was so short—I didn't want to waste time sweating the small stuff and things I couldn't change. I wanted to focus on the things that made me happy and to change what I could. Life will be what you make it, so I started making it what I wanted it to be. I started affirming and speaking greatness once more.

My oncologist scheduled me for an appointment to get a port put in. Everything went great. I was able to heal for about a week and a half before I went in for the new treatment protocol.

I was a little nervous on treatment day, but I stood fast on God's word. I said, "God, you have not given me a spirit of fear, but of power, love and a sound mind." I had to speak God's word to myself a lot. That's what He gave it to us for, to remind Him of what He said and to apply it to our lives. That is what kept me. I prayed over that medicine before it went into my veins and I tried my best not to worry. I had to let go and let God and the medicine do their job.

As I was sitting there getting my treatment, God said, "Put your words on a shirt."

I heard that so clear. I said, "Alright God. I will do just that." But I didn't know what to do after that. I prayed and God reminded me of this guy I used to work with that did t-shirts. I called him and asked him if he would be able to do some shirts for me.

"I am trying to start a t-shirt business and I would love your help," I told him. I gave him my motto, and he later sent me a sample on the shirt. We went back and forth until I was satisfied with the final product and I ordered twenty shirts to start off. I didn't want to order a bulk of shirts and have a boat load of inventory left behind. But I was surprised by the people who ordered shirts and supported me. I had to reorder more.

After a while, things slowed down, and I had quite a few shirts left over. T-shirts are a seasonal business, so I had to expect a time of no activity, just like any other business. I wasn't going to give up on it though. I thoroughly enjoyed it. My plan is to expand soon, with more sayings, a website, and sales. After all, I do like to operate in a spirit of excellence.

I am excited for what God is doing. He gave me a vision when I was going through my first chemo treatment in 2008. I had an idea to create a shoe case and a luggage line. I did my best to sketch my vision on paper, but it looked like a ten-year-old did it. Years down the road, God sent my cousin who lived in Germany at the time. She came to live with me for a year because she wanted to see what it was like to attend school in the states. Little did I know she was an artist. I couldn't believe it. I asked her if she could sketch my luggage if I gave her my vision. She said, "Sure, I can try." And she did just that. I couldn't believe when she finished, it was just how I envisioned it. I was amazed. The downside to this is, it's still sitting on paper. I believe God will someday allow this to manifest, but until then, I will focus on my shirts and trust God to send someone to help me with my luggage and shoe case.

But this wasn't everything God had for me. One Sunday, at church, one of our elders, Andrea Hines, stopped me and asked to talk to me after church. When I met with her, she said, "I have been in prayer for a while, and I have been looking for someone to bless with their own radio show on my broadcast network, and God said, 'Monique!'"

I couldn't believe it. I had chills up and down my arms and I said, "What? Are you serious?"

"Yes! I have been praying and God said you! So, I am offering you the opportunity to have your own radio show!"

I said, "YES!" and hugged her. I was so humbled that God would speak my name to Elder Hines and give me the opportunity and a platform to share with others.

It was in September 2019 when that awesome news was presented to me. I did my first show in October. I was a nervous wreck. I was new to this and didn't know anything about being a host. I was used to sharing inspiration with people on Facebook, that was it! After the show ended, I started to talk myself out of it.

"Can I really do this? This might be a little too much for me. God, I don't know enough people to interview."

You name it, I used it as an excuse and tried to renege afterward. I felt a little scared and that this might be too big of a job for me. I already felt like I was a woman with not many words. I was quiet and didn't talk much. What in the world was I going to do with a radio show on ALH Broadcasting, an affiliate of the Streaming Inspirational Broadcast Network!

We had bumps in the road in the beginning, and I was discouraged. I told myself, "Maybe this is a sign that this is not for me." But God didn't tell me anything about letting this opportunity go, so I stayed and continued to do it even though I was afraid. I don't know why I was scared to go forth, but I was. As time went on, things seemed to get a little easier, and I felt like I was getting the hang of being a host of an internet radio show. I would record more than one show to have as a Plan B just in case I wasn't feeling well because I was going through chemo treatments and didn't feel my best all the time.

In the middle of November, I was now around seven shows in, and I wasn't feeling well. Thank God for the shows I had recorded previously. I had a cough that wouldn't go away. I developed a low-grade fever the next day, so I started taking some Tylenol and Advil to try and break it. But my fever stayed a little above 102. Two days passed, and I called my doctor. It was about 2 am, so I had to speak with the on-call doctor. I asked him, "When should I go to the doctor with a fever?"

"With you having cancer, if your fever is at 100.1, you need to go to the hospital," he said.

"I will go when daybreak gets here, if it does not go down."

The next day came and my fever was down to 99.6, so I relaxed and just stayed in the bed. Although my fever was down, I still felt horrible in my head and in my body. I felt so tired, and drained. My son was home with me, so he made me some soup and tried to keep me hydrated. Evening came and I started feeling bad. I took my temperature, and it was 103! I told my son to take me to the hospital.

When we arrived, they triaged me. After a while they let me know that they were going to be running tests and doing a CT Scan. They also said they wanted to swab me to see if I had the flu. They took that long Q-Tip and stuck it way back into my nose. It felt like they swabbed my brain. I jumped and moved the nurse's hand away from my nose. She was not happy with me.

"Please don't do that. You can damage something. We are going to have to swab again because of your moving. We couldn't get anything the first time."

I wanted to tell her, "Forget it, don't do it again! I don't have the flu, I had the shot around a month prior," but I did it anyway. I then went to get scans done of my chest and was wheeled back and given more fever reducing meds. They hooked me up to an IV. After around an hour or so, the doctor came back in and said, "Well, you're good. You don't have the flu! But you will be admitted because you have a bad case of pneumonia."

"Pneumonia," I repeated.

"Because you have the fever, we are keeping you to get that under control, and now treat the pneumonia. He showed me the CT Scan and showed me that my whole right lung was just about covered.

I stayed in the hospital for a week. I was miserable. At one point, I thought I was going to die. I also had bad coughing spells. One night, I coughed so much that my diaphragm became weak. I could barely take another breath to let a cough out. I was in the bathroom and told Tyrell to call the nurse. I was so scared. It felt like my legs were getting ready to buckle and I was going to pass out. The nurse came in, helped me out of the bathroom, told me to sit on the bed and try to take some deep breaths. They gave me a breathing treatment. I had never been so scared in my life.

So much went on during those seven days; I was just ready to go home. My fever broke after the fifth day of being there. Then I developed sepsis. It was just ongoing and felt like it was never going to end. I prayed and prayed for God to heal me and allow me to walk up out of that hospital. I had breathing treatments and exercises to do until the last day of my hospital stay. My pulmonologist came in from time to time to check on me and update me with my progress. He was the one who let me know I was going to be discharged that day. My fever had been down for two days in a row, and I could continue medications at home for the pneumonia. I was so happy to hear those words. He asked me to follow up with him in two weeks to get a chest x-ray done to make sure things were still clearing up. I know Tyrell was happy. He slept on a chair that converted into a so-called bed for seven days. My husband would come in the day sometimes so that Tyrell could go home and rest in his own bed for several hours. But then he would come right back to the hospital to be with his mom.

After I was released from the hospital, a week later, Tyrell came down with pneumonia. I really think we had COVID-19 then (I think it was here in November or December), but we all recovered.

# Chapter 20

It was now a new month and I was excited because my sister was coming down to spend some time with me now that I was out of the hospital. My sister reminds me so much of our mother and she enjoys cooking, something I don't like to do.

Well, my sister arrived the following week, and she came with me to my follow-up appointment with my pulmonologist. He was such a nice man. I had not been in the presence of a doctor with such a sweet spirit in a long time. He actually cared and was genuinely concerned. He went over everything and took his time with me. He told me that the pneumonia wasn't quite gone yet. The cough might linger, and it might take another month or two before I was better. He asked me if I had a CPAP machine.

"Yes, I do," I told him, and then added, "Though I don't use it like I should."

"Well, start using it every night."

I asked him if he was a sleep doctor as well, and he said yes. I told him I would be leaving my sleep study center and he would be my new sleep study doctor.

"Do you know that you have early-stage emphysema/COPD?" he then asked me. I was a little taken aback when he said that, but then I remembered my Primary Care Physician telling me that years ago when I had an appointment with him. He mentioned emphysema then, but he didn't say anything about COPD. Things had apparently progressed a little over the years and now had turned into Chronic Obstructive Pulmonary Disease. I did notice I get winded quick, but my prayer was that it didn't get any worse. It's a progressive disease, but also treatable. I didn't want it to get any further. When my doctor told me to start sleeping with my CPAP machine like I was supposed to, I told him I would.

"If you would like to see me from now on, we can arrange that, and I will see you back in six months."

July 2020 was the six-month anniversary of my diagnosis of Pneumonia. God healed me of that, and sepsis too. That was a very scary experience, and I would never want to go through that ever again.

With all that behind me, I was ready to get back to my radio show. I told God I wanted to have a theme song for my show, Tea Talk and Testimonies. He started dropping little verses in my spirit, and before you know it, I had a little opening song for my show. I couldn't believe I did it. I was so proud of myself. A good friend of mine added the music to it, and Bam! my little theme song to Tea Talk and Testimonies was birthed!

I did a show after being a month off with the pneumonia with just myself, no guest. I wanted to let my audience know why I was out for a month and thank them for sticking in there with me.

I am so grateful for all that God has brought me through. I believe greater is on the horizon. God is not through with me yet.

Just remember, when things seem impossible for you, all things are possible with God. He specializes in the impossible. Never give up, never give in. You are more than a conqueror through Christ Jesus.

I believe we all have a story to tell. With everything that I been through, I never allowed it to separate me from God. I know that He loves me and was there with me all the time. There are just some things we just have to go through, it's a part of life. Allow God to turn your trials into triumphs and your mess into a message. There are people waiting on us, they need to hear our stories about how God brought us through. I believe that's what God has done and continues to do for me. He will do the same for you. Let God work a miracle in your life. Give your life to Him. That is one decision you will never regret.

I love you all and I pray that something in this book will help you keep pressing on and never lose hope. If we don't understand anything else about God, know that He is sovereign. Selah...God Bless. Remember to keep a smile on our face and a hello in your mouth. It just might change a person's day.

Take the limits off and....

#LIVELIFELIMITLESS
#BEFREEANDSOAR

Monique Headecker-Green

# More Information

Those suffering from cancer can reach out to the American Cancer Society at 1-800-227-2345. They have a lot of great programs and services.

Those in domestic violence situations can reach out to the National Domestic Violence Hotline at 1-800-799-SAFE.

If you find yourself suffering with mental illness like depression and anxiety, don't be afraid to reach out to a licensed therapist in your area for help.

# Acknowledgements

First and foremost, I want to thank God for believing in me when I didn't believe in myself, seeing in me what I was not able to see in myself, and keeping me when I thought I couldn't make it or keep myself.

To my Bishop Ronald and Pastor Karla Godbee, thank you for loving me and my family, and for always keeping us covered in prayer. I am forever grateful to you for walking with me through my journey and sharing much wisdom with me through my fight to live. Thank you for always inspiring me to exercise my faith and put it to work when I didn't receive great news from the doctors. Thank you for your great teachings that have caused my faith to be elevated to a place I never thought it would be.

To Pastors Steve and Valerie Sims, thank you for everything!

To Pastor Kelvin, thank you for visiting me in the hospital when I was sick.

To all the Elders, Pastors, Deacons, and my whole River Family, thank you for always showing love towards me. I am forever grateful.

To Bishop Nellie Harris and the entire Matthew Chapel Church Family, thank you for continuing to love me after all these years, and fighting right alongside with me again for a second time of this cancer journey. Thank you, Bishop, for always saying, "You got this!" Thank you for your continued prayers. I was so happy to know that people cared and wanted to make sure I was alright and didn't need for anything.

Thank you, John and Diane Denning for great fellowship and blessed opportunities offered to us.

To Apostle Debra Brown. Thank you for always keeping me before the Lord and helping me see things differently. Thank you for allowing my husband and I to be a part of your life, for the many days we've broken bread together and sat at your table with you and fellowshipped. Thank you for entrusting me to be a part of your private life and for us sharing many moments of ups and downs. I cannot thank you enough for being there for me through some pretty rough moments in my life. Because of you, I have now learned to say, "It is well with my soul."

# About the Author

Monique (Nikki) Headecker-Green is a native New Yorker currently residing in the wonderful city of Raleigh, North Carolina, where she's lived for the past twenty-five years. She is a wife and a mother of two sons and a fur baby daughter. She went to school to become a medical assistant and an EMT in New York and a

Veterinary Technician in North Carolina. In 2002, she started working at the Employment Security Commission, where she was employed for fifteen years until she received a Stage IV Metastatic Breast Cancer diagnosis. Even though this is her second battle fighting cancer (most recent a Terminal Stage IV diagnosis), she is thriving every day, trusting, and believing that the God she serves holds her life in His hands. She'll be the first to tell you her time is when God says, not man. After her separation from the Employment Security Commission, she started treatment, became a radio/internet talk show host on ALH Broadcasting, an affiliate of the Streaming Inspirational Broadcast Network, and started her beaded jewelry line. She lives in the present and enjoys every day she is alive.